The Zoroastrian Faith

D0094405

The Zoroastrian Faith

Tradition and Modern Research

S. A. NIGOSIAN

McGill-Queen's University Press
Montreal & Kingston•London•Buffalo

© McGill-Queen's University Press 1993
ISBN 0-7735-1133-4 (cloth)
ISBN 0-7735-1144-X (paper)

Legal deposit third quarter 1993
Bibliothèque nationale du Québec

Printed in Canada on acid-free paper

This book has been published with the help of a grant
from the Canadian Federation for the Humanities,
using funds provided by the Social Sciences and
Humanities Research Council of Canada.
Publication has also been supported by the Canada
Council through its block grant program.

Canadian Cataloguing in Publication Data

Nigosian, S. A.
    The Zoroastrian faith: tradition and modern
    research
    Includes bibliographical reference and index.
    ISBN 0-7735-1133-4 (bound)
    ISBN 0-7735-1144-X (pbk.)
    1. Zoroastrianism. I. Title.
    BL1571.N44 1993   295   C93-090211-4

To
Hrant Bardakjian for one reason
and
Berge Papazian for another

Contents

Acknowledgments

Short extracts from translations of various texts are acknowledged as follows:

Zand Akâsîh, Iranian or Greater Bundahisn, trans. by Behramgore T. Anklesaria, Copyright © 1956, Rahnumae Mazdasna Sabha.

Purity and Pollution in Zoroastrianism: Triumph Over Evil, by Jamsheed K. Choksy, Copyright © 1989, University of Texas Press.

The Zend Avesta, trans. by James Darmesteter and L.H. Mills, Copyright © 1880, Oxford University Press.

The Gathas of Zarathushtra, trans. by Stanley Insler, Copyright © 1975, E.J. Brill.

Old Persian Grammar, Texts, Lexicon, 2nd. ed., trans. by Roland G. Kent, Copyright © 1953, American Oriental Society.

An Introduction to Ancient Iranian Religion: Readings from the Avesta and Achaemenid Inscriptions, by William W. Malandra, Copyright © 1983, University of Minnesota Press.

The Wisdom of the Sasanian Sages (Denkard VI), trans. by Shaul Shaked, Copyright © 1979, Westview Press.

Pahlavi Texts, trans. by Edward W. West, Copyright © 1880, Oxford University Press.

Preface

Anyone familiar with the Zoroastrian faith must realize the difficulties and uncertainties inherent in the study of its essential aspects. Questions surrounding the contribution of Zoroaster, the spread of his faith, and the development of his teachings and practices are not easy to deal with; in spite of painstaking scholarly research in the field of Zoroastrian (and Iranian) ethnology, philology, archaeology, and history, there is still hardly any concrete evidence by which one can trace precisely the faith's origin and development. In fact, the ambiguous nature of the linguistic evidence, the lack of a proper philological and exegetical tradition to the Zoroastrian scriptures, the gaps in the historical sources, and the contradictions in the existing records defy a precise historical reconstruction. But these difficulties and uncertainties (duly noted and treated in the text) should in no way prevent us from presenting an instructive analytical work on the Zoroastrian faith.

The first chapter consists of the following: the historical background of the world into which Zoroaster appeared, the principal sources of information concerning Zoroaster, and both the traditional account and the opinion of modern scholars concerning his life and teachings. This is followed in Chapter Two by a description of the historical development and spread of Zoroastrianism from its origin to the present day, even though the paucity and varied nature of the sources make it difficult to trace precisely the development of the faith. Also included in this second chapter is a section on the religious conflict between Zoroastrian and non-Zoroastrian faiths during the Sasanid dynasty.

Chapter Three presents a description of the collection of Zoroastrian sacred writings (including the history of the Avesta), the various versions (Pahlavi and Sanskrit), and several important religious documents, all of which are illustrated by a number of selections. Chapter Four analyzes the basic Zoroastrian beliefs and concepts, including the worship of one supreme God, the veneration of lesser divine beings, the importance of the personal choice to struggle against Satan, the destruction of the world, individual resurrection and judgment, eternal life and bliss, and the matter of the influence of these teachings on Judaism, Christianity, and Islam. Finally, Chapter Five describes the prescribed Zoroastrian rituals and observances, from birth to death. A glossary and bibliography are provided as aids for further study.

Scholarly research is not an isolated endeavour. Hence, it is a pleasure to acknowledge my debt of gratitude to a number of friends and colleagues who read all or part of the manuscript and provided helpful comments and criticisms. I wish in particular to thank Prof. Ted Lutz, Prof. Ferhang Mehr, Yazdi Antia, Homi Homji, and two anonymous reviewers.

I am also grateful to my friend and colleague Alan Davies for his unflagging interest in my ideas and for his constant support and encouragement; to Donald Akenson of McGill-Queen's University Press for his interest in the book and for his commitment to seeing it through to publication; to June Hewitt for her meticulous preparation of the typescript as it emerged in various stages; to Eleanor Murphy for rearranging the final draft according to the required house style; to Catherine Marjoribanks for her careful editing of the manuscript; to Debbie van Eeken for sorting out various bits of pertinent information and for preparing the index; and to the members of Victoria College for their generous assistance in providing all the necessary facilities.

This opportunity cannot be passed without expressing my special thanks to Henaz for her love, dedication, and sacrifice.

The Zoroastrian Faith

CHAPTER ONE

Zoroaster

A tiny ethno-religious community of Zoroastrians (also known as Mazdayasnians, or Mazda-worshippers) profess to follow today the faith once propagated by their prophet, Zoroaster, who lived and taught in ancient Persia (modern Iran) sometime before the rise of the Achaemenid dynasty (ca. 550 BCE – precise dates for Zoroaster are unknown). A small group of Zoroastrians still live in their ancient homeland in modern Iran. Other Zoroastrians migrated from Iran during the ninth and tenth centuries CE and settled on the west coast of India. Their number at present is still small, and they are popularly known as Parsees (or Parsis) – a name that refers to the province of Fars in ancient Persia. Since the rise of European imperialism, Zoroastrians from both Iran and India have emigrated and established small communities in almost every major city in the West.

This exposure to western influence has deeply affected the adherents of the Zoroastrian faith. Like most other faiths, Zoroastrianism is subject to the irresistible transforming power of western ideas, particularly those of agnosticism and scepticism. Ancient customs are being questioned and traditional patterns are being threatened. As a result, conservative and reformist forces are in conflict, with neither side winning a clear victory.

Who was Zoroaster, and what did he teach? Before answering these questions it is necessary to present a brief historical background of the world into which Zoroaster appeared.

THE WORLD OF ZOROASTER

One of the most important areas for the study of human history is the Middle East – the region popularly called "the cradle of ancient civilizations." Here, a number of ancient and modern peoples – the Egyptians, the Babylonians, the Assyrians, the Medes, the Persians, the Greeks, the Romans, the Arabs, and the Turks – built great empires and imposed their will upon the territory's inhabitants. To be sure, there is hardly any racial, political, or linguistic homogeneity in the Middle East. And yet, modern Middle Easterners share a deep sense of pride in the history of their great past, particularly in their pioneering contributions of such fundamental innovations as agriculture; the domestication of animals for food, clothing, and transportation; spinning and weaving; irrigation and drainage; standard tools and weapons; the wheel and metal-works; symbols of writing and keeping of records; astronomical observation and the calendar; mathematics; abstract thought; and many religious ideas and symbols.

The earliest historical period of the Middle East is characterized by rivalries and struggles for supremacy and domination among the various groups of people occupying the area. A number of city-states coalesced, either by force or by persuasion, to form a large political unit. Egypt was the first in Middle Eastern civilization to achieve such a political unification by about 3000 BCE under the rule of King Menes (or Narmer). Egypt's history from that point up to the Persian domination in the sixth century BCE changed very little, though internal disorders and external groups (such as the Hyksos, the Nubians, the Ethiopians, and the Assyrians) occasionally disrupted this unity. Native Egyptian dynasties continued to reassert themselves politically.

Moreover, by means of numerous campaigns or alliances, the Egyptians were capable of extending their power eastward to Mesopotamia (modern Iraq), northward to Asia Minor (modern Turkey-Syria), westward to present-day Libya, and southward to Nubia (modern Sudan). Egyptian trade and commerce with foreign ports was well developed. Similarly, Egyptian architecture, art, craftsmanship, and metalwork were not only well advanced but among the best in the ancient world. Also, they introduced, in the third millennium BCE, a calendar with a solar year of 365 days. Their most lasting and outstanding achievements, however, were the massive royal tombs (known as the Pyramids), the Sphinx (part of a massive mortuary temple connected with the Pyramid tomb), and the temples of Luxor and Karnak.

The history of Mesopotamia (modern Iraq) during this period is completely different from Egypt's. Here, the territory was exposed to continual invasions, and no significant unity was achieved (except for brief periods by neo-Assyrian and neo-Babylonian empires) until the Persian conquest in the sixth century BCE. During most of the twenty-four hundred years from the thirtieth to the sixth century BCE a succession of governments, differing politically and sometimes ethnically, developed what is called a "Mesopotamian" civilization.

The group of people living in southern Mesopotamia by 3000 BCE were the Sumerians. Their racial and linguistic origins are uncertain, but much of their culture, including their invention of writing, was absorbed by succeeding civilizations. About 2300 BCE, Sargon I, a Semitic ruler of a nearby city (Akkad or Agade), revolted against the Sumerians and conquered their territory. Sargon was one of the Semitic nomads who periodically migrated from the desert expanses of Arabia to the Tigris-Euphrates valley. He founded the dynasty of Akkad and established his capital in Babylon (modern Karbala). He and his Akkadian successors succeeded in controlling and unifying the region, including some adjacent territories. During his dynastic rule, trading expeditions extended from Asia Minor to India.

Over a century later, the Gutians, a mountain people living in the region of Kurdistan, invaded southern Mesopotamia and disestablished the Akkadian dynasty. But Gutian control, too, came to an end after only a century when the Sumerians re-emerged under the new dynasty of the celebrated leader Ur-Nammu. Under his rule a highly organized empire and an extensive system of centralized control developed. The two most striking legacies of Ur-Nammu's reign were the ziggurat, a great, rectangular, stepped tower some seventy feet high erected in honour of Nanna, the moon god, and a legal "code," the earliest collection of laws now known.

Several centuries later, the influx of another Semitic group known as the Amorites (or Amurru), the ever-recurring raids of the Elamites (perhaps of Alpine race), and internal racial rebellions finally crushed this neo-Sumerian empire. The result was the establishment of city-states governed by various Semitic tribes (mainly Elamite and Amorite) for nearly two centuries. Then around 1800 BCE Hammurabi came to power. A commanding leader and a capable administrator, he succeeded where others had failed. He welded the fragmented city-states of Mesopotamia into one kingdom known as the Babylonian dynasty. He gave the entire region one legal system, known as the "Code of Hammurabi," and one language, the Akkadian (old Babylonian) language.

Although this sociological pattern imposed by Hammurabi continued for several centuries, his military achievements did not long survive him. Once again, incursions of Indo-European tribes from beyond the Caucasus Mountains southward into Mesopotamia caused a great confusion.

The first group of invaders to strike Mesopotamia, shortly before 1600 BCE, were the Kassites, who eventually established a dynasty that ruled most of south and south-east Mesopotamia for several centuries. Other groups that conquered north-west Mesopotamia and were able to hold it in subjection for a few centuries were the Hittites and the Mitannis. The Hittites had invaded Asia Minor several centuries before; now, during their expansion south-eastward, they sacked and looted the Babylonian capital. The Mitannis ruled a large, feudalistic area in Tell Halaf (in the vicinity of modern Syria-Armenia) where previously the Hurrians had been settled. And to add insult to injury, the Egyptians claimed south-western Mesopotamia and obtained tribute for a few centuries. Relations between these confederations were governed by elaborate treaties, which were constantly broken.

The ultimate beneficiary of all these confederations, or city-states, was destined to be the Assyrians, an insignificant Semitic tribe from Ashur (or Assur) in northern Mesopotamia. Meanwhile, the thirteenth century BCE saw the irruptive appearance of new peoples in the Middle East. The best known of the new settlers from the west were the Phrygians, the Lydians, and the Philistines.

For some time the Phrygians occupied most of the old Hittite area in Asia Minor, but later, in the seventh century BCE, they were defeated by the Lydians. The Philistines, who are considered to have come from the Aegean Islands (or, according to another account, from Crete), occupied the south coast of Canaan (Palestine, or modern Lebanon-Israel). They captured Canaanite cities and established a strong confederation of city-states. Nonetheless, they were constantly at war with surrounding tribes, especially the Israelites.

The Israelite invasion and settlement of Canaan around the thirteenth century BCE, inspired by their vision of the "Promised Land," coincided with the Philistine invasion and colonization of the same territory. Their timing could not have been much worse. It was little wonder, then, that their struggle to establish an independent Israelite kingdom was so hard fought.

The conquest of virtually all of Canaan by the Israelites did not become a reality until David's reign in the tenth century BCE. King David captured Jerusalem and expanded his territory to control everything from Syria to the Arabian desert, and from the Mediterranean Sea to the borders of Mesopotamia. However, this Israelite monarchy did not last very long. A little less than a century after its establishment it split into two. The northern part was destroyed by the Assyrians in the eighth century BCE. The southern part survived for a while, but eventually it too succumbed to the Chaldeans (also known as neo-Babylonians) in the sixth century BCE.

Assyrian militarism brought unity and even a degree of peace to the Middle East, but it was a peace based on terror. Once Assyrian leadership faltered, the empire collapsed. The coalition of Medes and Chaldeans destroyed the power of Assyria for all time to come. Nineveh, the capital of Assyria, fell in 612 BCE, and its site remains desolate to this day.

Meanwhile, a new power was emerging in Persia. After defeating Media and uniting various tribes, a new Persian leader, Cyrus II (559–529 BCE), led his army victoriously into Asia Minor. During the subsequent decade Cyrus conducted an astonishing series of military campaigns. His empire stretched from India through Mesopotamia to Syria-Canaan.

Questions concerning the historical roots and development of the Persians are still unresolved. All that can be said is that the Persians were a group of Indo-Aryans who ruled a vast territory in the Middle East for over a thousand years, from about 550 BCE to 651 CE. But the subject of the arrival and settlement of the Indo-Aryans in Iran is still a matter for dispute.[1] It is generally held that the Medes and the Persians were the two groups of Aryans (from whom the term "Aryana" or "Iran" derives) who occupied and settled in the territory of Iran in the course of several centuries and in subsequent waves shortly after 1500 BCE.

The first Aryan people to make an impact in west Asia were the Medes. Sometime around the eighth century BCE they conquered the Urartu in the north, the Hittites in the west, and the Assyrians in the south and became the greatest power in west Asia. The formation of a Median confederation or state began when a certain chieftain called Daiukku (GK Deioces) devised a plan in 716 BCE for the union of certain tribal chiefs. But around this time the Cimmerians and the Scythians, warlike, nomadic peoples, appeared on the scene and caused serious disturbances. It was 673 BCE before Kashtaritu (OP Khshathrita, GK Phraortes) reformed a united Median state. Kashtaritu was soon defeated, but with the rise of Cyaxares, the united Median power grew greater than ever before, and the Persians, now in Persis, submitted to the Medes. A century later, however, the Medes lost their power and became subject to the Persians.

The Persians traced their history back to a certain eponymous ancestor called Achaemenes. But it was Cyrus II, a fifth-generation descendant of Achaemenes and a young prince of Fars (GK Persis, from which the term "Parsee" and "Persian" derive), who overthrew the Medes in 550 BCE and established the Achaemenid dynasty (550–330 BCE). In a short time he invaded the entire west Asian territory, from the borders of India to Greece. This extensive empire, consisting of widely differing peoples, cultures, and religious traditions, was held together by Cyrus's innovative policy. He broke the tradition of victor as despoiler and avenger. Instead of invoking fire, the sword, the mass deportation of whole populations, and the rigorous suppression of all nationalistic aspirations, he conceded to the vanquished a high degree of cultural and political autonomy, including religious freedom. In other words, he accepted existing institutions almost without modifications; he respected local traditions and adapted himself to them; and he honoured the gods of all the people within his domain.

Cyrus was succeeded by his son Cambyses II (529–522 BCE), who continued his father's work of conquest by adding Egypt and the Greek islands of Cyprus and Samos. Before his death, the throne was taken by a Magian usurper called Gaumata, who claimed to be Bardiya (GK Smerdis), the brother of Cambyses (cf. Herodotus 3.61–79). But who were the Magi(ans)?

The problem of identifying the Magi(ans) is exceedingly difficult.[2] To begin with, the etymology of the word (OP *magu*, GK *magos*) is unclear. Then, the available sources (archaeological, inscriptional, literary) provide a confusing image regarding the character or activities of the Magi. It is possible that originally they arose from the priestly caste of the Medes. Later, under the Achaemenids, they performed certain rituals and ceremonies connected with fire, sacrifices, and burials (cf. Herodotus 1.101, 107, 132, 140). Still later, possibly after the contact with the Greeks and continuing up to the Islamic period, they may have claimed the possession of supernatural knowledge and acted as fortune-tellers, astrologers, magicians, sorcerers, tricksters, and charlatans. Thus, though their long survival testifies to their vitality, little is known about the development of or the role played by the Magians.

Returning then to Gaumata, his reign lasted only six months, at which time Darius I (522–486 BCE), son of Vishtaspa (GK Hystaspes) and a member of the Achaemenid dynasty, succeeded in securing the throne for himself after killing the Magians (cf. Herodotus 3.79). Next he put down a wave of rebellion throughout the empire. Then he crossed the Bosphorus in 512 BCE, subdued Thrace, and crossed the Danube River, but withdrew without consolidating these gains. Later, revolts in the Greek colonies of Asia Minor led him in 493 BCE and again in 491 BCE to fight against Greece, but in the end he was forced to withdraw to Asia Minor following the Battle of Marathon.

The political structure of the Persian empire reached its fullest development under Darius the Great. It consisted of an absolute hereditary monarchy assisted by a central council of nobles and represented in the imperial provinces by local governors called satraps. In time, however, this political efficiency was overcome by corruption and civil strife, and the earlier policy of tolerance gave way to repression. The result was the gradual loss of confidence and alienation of subject peoples.

Xerxes I (486–465 BCE) succeeded his father Darius I and led another campaign against Greece. In 480 BCE he captured and burned Athens. But the defeat of his Persian fleet at the Battle of Salamis forced him to withdraw, and the loss of his cavalry at the Battle of Platea the next year consolidated the Greek victory.

Artaxerxes I (465–425 BCE) followed his father and reigned for forty years. During his reign, internal decay within the Achaemenid empire appeared in the form of revolts, first in Egypt and then in other satrapies. Also, intermittent warfare with the Greek states continued for a long time. Not until the accession of Artaxerxes III (359–338 BCE) were the earlier boundaries of the Achaemenid empire re-established for a brief period. The empire finally came to an end during the reign of Darius III (336–331 BCE), at the hands of Alexander the Great.

Alexander of Macedonia (356–323 BCE) first established control over the Greek mainland before setting out against Persia. In the spring of 334 BCE, he stormed into Asia Minor with an army of 35,000 men, marched along the Mediterranean coast into Syria, then turned north and captured Darius's wife and mother. Next, he marched south into Phoenicia (modern Lebanon and Israel), captured Tyre, and conquered Gaza. When he arrived in Egypt, the Egyptians hailed him as a deliverer, because they hated their harsh Persian rulers.

Then, Alexander turned once again to the Persian front. He met Darius III and his Persian army east of the Tigris River near the plain of Arbela (close to the city of Gaugamela) and in a decisive battle forced Darius III and his army to retire to the east. Darius III fled and was later killed by one of his generals, leaving Alexander king of Asia.

Babylon surrendered and Alexander entered the Persian heartland. He captured the city of Susa; burned the city of Persepolis in retaliation for the Persian burning of Athens; marched southward occupying all the region ruled by local tribesmen; then turned northward to Afghanistan, Bactria, Sogdiana, and the Hindu Kush mountains until he reached the rich plains of India in 326 BCE. The realm of Alexander now stretched from the Ionian Sea to the borders of north India. In 323 BCE, on the eve of an expedition to conquer Arabia, he fell ill and died at the age of thirty-three.

Sometime during these dramatic and decisive events Zoroaster appeared. But who was Zoroaster? When and where was he born?

PRINCIPAL SOURCES

Of all the great religious founders, Zoroaster is certainly one of the least known. This statement may come as a surprise to those who are not experts in Zoroastrian literary criticism. But every scholar who has tried to study the mass of traditions preserved in the Zoroastrian texts knows that the endeavour to sift the evidence to arrive at some tangible historical facts results only in the most unpleasant feeling of uncertainty, because the available sources of information provide conflicting images of the prophet.

The principal sources on Zoroaster may be classified under two categories: Zoroastrian and non-Zoroastrian. The Zoroastrian sources of information consist of the Avesta (the Zoroastrian scripture, which contains the Yasna, Visparad, Videvdat, and the Yashts) and a collection of later religious documents (such as the Bundahishn, Denkard, Zadspram, and many more). The non-Zoroastrian sources of information are found in works by classical authors, mainly Greek and Roman, and references by Armenian, Syrian, Arab, Chinese, and Icelandic writers.

Naturally, these diverse sources of information are not all of equal importance, even though each has a certain intrinsic value. The Avesta, and in particular the Gathas (hymns) of Zoroaster (Yasna 28–34, 43–51, 53), stands foremost in importance. The classical references, as a rule, rank next to the Avesta, while the information provided in the remaining sources is especially valuable to substantiate the statements presented in both the Avesta and the classical writings.

While the Avesta may retain certain essential features of the original teachings, it is believed to have derived its authority from "faithfully preserved" older traditions. How much of its contents dates from the earliest period, and how much of it was re-written to make the past agree with the realities and beliefs of the time in which it was composed is, of course, open to question. In fact, the surviving Avesta is only a fragment of the whole, and the disparity of its parts is evidence of the vicissitudes through which it went before it became crystallized to its present form.

The Gathas are considered to contain the life and teachings of Zoroaster himself, but unfortunately their archaic language creates an enormous difficulty in eliciting meaning from the obscure texts. This is best illustrated by comparing the translations of the Gathas made by several competent scholars, whose differences are quite startling.

The information preserved in the later Zoroastrian sources are usually considered to be the natural continuation of the Avesta. But here, too, the ambiguity of the scripts, and the legendary material that has accrued through the centuries, create a difficulty in reconstructing the life of Zoroaster with any degree of certainty. In fact, the incongruities in the existing records have resulted in diverse opinions among scholars on almost every aspect of Zoroaster's life. So, before considering the major difficulties presented by the available sources, it will be useful to present the traditional (and popular) view of Zoroaster.

ZOROASTER IN TRADITION

Zoroastrian tradition maintains that Zoroaster was a prophet of ancient Iran who lived in the seventh to sixth centuries BCE. His birthplace was Azerbaijan, north-west of Media. His father, Pourushaspa, was from the family of Spitama, whose genealogy is traced back through forty-five generations to Gayomart, the first man (like Adam), and his mother, Dughdhova, was from the clan of Hvogva (Yasna 46.13, 51.12, 53.1). Of his mother, it is said that at the age of fifteen she conceived and gave virgin birth to Zoroaster.

The traditional account of Zoroaster's infancy and later life abounds with miracles. He is said to have been born laughing, instead of weeping (Denkard 7.3.2). He is also said to have escaped as an infant numerous attempts made on his life, through the intervention of beasts (Denkard 7.3.8 ff.). First, a bull stood over him to protect him from the hoofs of cattle; then a stallion saved him in the same way from being trampled by horses; and again, a she-wolf accepted him among her cubs, instead of devouring him. (Stories of such nature are not taken seriously by a group of modern Zoroastrians.)

Tradition, furthermore, maintains that Zoroaster was trained to be a priest (Yasna 33.6, 13.94). At the age of twenty, however, Zoroaster left home, against the wishes of his parents (Zadspram 16.1). Ten years later, his quest for truth culminated in a vision, or revelation (Yasna 43; Denkard 7.3.51; Zadspram 21.1–27). The story of this first vision, as stated in Zoroastrian tradition, is as follows (Zadspram 20–21). Zoroaster was attending the celebration of the spring festival and, according to ancient custom, fetched water at dawn from a nearby river for a sacred ritual. As he returned to the bank from mid-river, he saw the shining figure of the archangel Vohu Mana (Good Intention), who led Zoroaster to the presence of Ahura Mazda (Wise Lord) and the five Immortals, where he was taught the cardinal principles of the "true" or "good" religion. This vision, in which Zoroaster saw, heard, or felt conscious of Ahura Mazda, was later repeated a number of times (Yasna 31.8, 33.6–7, 43.5). As a result, Zoroaster believed that he was commissioned by Ahura Mazda to preach the "good religion" (Yasna 44.11, 28.4).

Tradition states, moreover, that Zoroaster's mission started at the age of thirty, and during the next ten years he was successful in converting only one person, his cousin Maidhyoimah (Yasna 51.19; Yasht 13.95; Bundahishn 32.2; Zadspram 23.1–2). These long, discouraging years brought him into sharp conflict with the priests of his day. Bitterly disappointed by their obduracy, he cried in despair to Ahura Mazda:

To what land to flee? Where shall I go to flee? They exclude (me) from my family and from my clan. The community with which I have associated has not satisfied me, nor those who are the deceitful rulers of the land. How, then, shall I satisfy Thee, Wise Lord? (Yasna 46.1)[3]

Suddenly a ray of hope flashed back in him as he triumphed in his own faith:

Yes, praising, I shall always worship all of you Wise Lord. (Yasna 50.4)[4]

Zoroaster's passionate concern for Ahura Mazda, his witnessing of the outrageous and shameless perversion of the religious rites, his utter despair at being deserted by kindred and fellow-workers, and his own inner doubts and questionings moved him deeply (Yasna 32.13–14, 46.2, 43.11, 49.1–2). Like the biblical leader Joshua (Joshua 24:15) and the prophet Micah (Micah 7:7), Zoroaster's words echoed triumphantly to haunt the imagination of human beings ever after:

I choose (only) thy teachings Lord. (Yasna 46.3)[5]

The tradition that perhaps remains the most popular among Zoro-astrians today is of Zoroaster's success in converting King Vishtaspa and the royal court in Bactria (Yasht 9.26, 13.99–100).[6] The story is that Zoroaster, after three days of disputations at a great assembly at the royal palace, encountered the hostility of the *kavis* and *karapans* (priests, or possibly religious leaders?). These enemies arranged for Zoroaster to be cast into prison, where he remained until he won the willing ear of King Vishtaspa by curing the king's favourite horse, who was paralysed (Denkard 7.4.70 ff.). Accordingly, King Vishtaspa, the queen, and all the royal dignitaries accepted whole-heartedly Zoroaster's teachings. This event, which, according to Zoroastrian tradition, took place when Zoroaster was forty-two years old, helped the spread of his faith.

Although the problems associated with the sources make it diffi-cult, if not impossible, to describe the spread of Zoroaster's teach-ings, there is some evidence that Zoroaster organized, perhaps in an informal way, a fellowship or brotherhood of his followers, and that this brotherhood had certain divisions within it (Yasna 32.1, 33.3, 46.1, 49.7). The three grades of his disciples were: the Xvaetu (Strong in Spirit), the Verezena (Fellow-worker), and the Airyamna (Friend).

Again, here and there certain names are mentioned, such as Maid-hyomaongha (Maidhyoimah, Medyomah), Paoruchista, Frashaoshtra, and Havovi (Yasna 28.7–8, 51.19, 53.3, 51.17). According to later (Pahlavi) tradition, Maidhyomaongha was Zoroaster's cousin and first disciple. Havovi, the sister of Frashaoshtra, was married to Zoroaster, and their youngest daughter, Paoruchista, married her uncle Jamaspa, brother of Havovi and Frashaoshtra. (This account is suggestive of incest and, therefore, refuted by modern Zoroas-trians.) Both brothers, Jamaspa and Frashaoshtra, had high posi-tions at the court of King Vishtaspa, Zoroaster's patron, who founded the first community of adherents (Yasna 29.11, 33.7, 44.11, 46.14, 51.16).

Furthermore, tradition states that Zoroaster lived in a new home, married three times (this polygamous marriage is rejected by mod-ern Zoroastrians), and had three sons and three daughters – three daughters and a son from the first wife, two sons from the second, and none from the third (Yasna 53.3; Yasht 13; Denkard 9.45; Great Bundahishn 35.56). His three sons initiated and represented the three classes of society: the priests, the warriors, and the farmers (Great Bundahishn 35.56; Indian Bundahishn 32.5). Finally, at the age of seventy-seven, Zoroaster died a violent death, though it is not known exactly how. One story is that he was assassinated while praying in the fire-temple; another states that he was slain with other priests in the fire-temple by the Turanians, who stormed the city of Balk (Denkard 5.3.2, 7.5.1; Dadistan i Dinik 72.8; Zadspram 23.9).

ZOROASTER IN MODERN RESEARCH

Although this traditional account may at first seem convincing, it is in no way free from difficulties. These obstacles become evident when an attempt is made to understand the meaning of his name, to resolve his place and date of birth, to determine his ancestry and family, or to outline his religious beliefs and teachings.

Name

The familiar form of the name Zoroaster derives from the Latin *Zoroastres*, which in turn is modelled after the Greek form *Zôrastrês*. In the Avesta, the name appears consistently as Zarathushtra, or in the full patronymic form as Zarathushtra Spitama. The Pahlavi version of the name is usually given as Zaratusht, and the modern Persian varieties are Zardusht, Zartusht, or Zarathust.

The precise etymology or significance of the name of Zoroaster remains uncertain. In classical antiquity, Zoroaster's name was thought to be associated with the Greek word *astrothutein*, meaning "star-worshipper."[7] In Syriac and Arabic writings, the name of Zoroaster was thought to have derived from two words, *zar washt*, meaning "golden kingdom" or "royal gold."[8] Other suggestions and explanations offered by earlier scholars for the name of Zoroaster include "bathed in gold," "melted silver," "gold-smith," "gold-stern," and "descendant of Ishtar/Venus." None of these explanations is considered acceptable at present. What is generally agreed is that the Avestan form of the name, Zarathushtra, consists of two compounds, namely *zarath* and *ushtra*, the latter meaning "camel" while the precise derivation and meaning of the former remains uncertain.[9] This has resulted in several propositions to explain the form of Zarathushtra: "he who can manage camels," "robbing a camel," "tormenting the camel," "old camel," "one whose camel is fierce," and so on.

As for the appelative Spitama, the term is considered a patronymic designation, possibly deriving from the Avestan root *spit*, meaning "brilliant," "aggressive," or "white." The significance would then be a "white descendant," or "having brilliance." Naturally, caution must be used in all such etymological explanations, because we do not possess sufficient linguistic data to enable us to be more precise in our explanation.

Dates

The diversity of opinion among scholars with reference to Zoroaster's dates is largely due to the incongruities of the existing records. The Avesta gives no direct information that might decisively fix Zoroaster's era.

The first group of writings to be considered are the classical references that place Zoroaster at a time earlier than 6000 BCE.[10] Diogenes Laertius (230 CE) says that, according to Xanthus of Lydia (ca. 450 BCE), Zoroaster lived six thousand years before the invasion of the Persian King Xerxes (ca. 480 BCE). This would date Zoroaster at about 6480 BCE. A variant reading in the text of Diogenes puts Zoroaster six hundred years before Xerxes, which would then place Zoroaster a little earlier than 1000 BCE. However, Diogenes also states that according to Hermodorus (ca. 400 BCE), Zoroaster lived five thousand years before the Trojan War (ca. 1200 BCE). In that case, Zoroaster lived around 6200 BCE. Plutarch (ca. 46–120 CE) too seems to support this last dating scheme for Zoroaster. Pliny the Elder (23–79 CE) cites Eudoxus (ca. 365 BCE) in placing Zoroaster six thousand years before the death of Plato (347 BCE), that is, around 6300 BCE. Needless to say, the sources that date Zoroaster at such an exaggeratedly early period are suspect and therefore unacceptable to critics.

A second group of references is found in the works of Arabic authors. Significantly enough, the Islamic author al-Biruni (973–1048) gives in his Arabic document *al-Athar-al-Bakiya* (*The Chronology of Ancient Nations*, written in 1000 CE) a precise date for Zoroaster. Al-Biruni states that "from his [i.e. Zoroaster's] appearance till the beginning of the era of Alexander, they count 258 years" (cf. Bundahishn 34.1–9; Arda Wiraz Namag 1.1–5; Denkard 7.7.6; Zadspram 33.11–12.).[11] How is this statement to be interpreted?

To the Iranians, "the beginning of the era of Alexander" signified the sack of Persepolis, the extinction of the Achaemenid empire, and the death of their last king, Darius III, in 330 BCE. In that case, Zoroaster's birth date would be 588 BCE. But what does al-Biruni mean by Zoroaster's appearance? Does he refer to Zoroaster's birth? In that case, Zoroaster's birth date would be 588 BCE. Or does he refer to Zoroaster's first appearance to the public after his visions at the age of thirty? Then Zoroaster's birth date would be 618 BCE. Or again, does he refer to the conversion of King Vishtaspa when Zoroaster was forty-two years old? Then Zoroaster's birth date would be 630 BCE. Actually, no matter how one wishes to interpret al-Biruni's statement, his precise date for Zoroaster is questionable because it seems simply to echo traditional Iranian belief, which by his time had little, if any, accurate knowledge of Zoroaster's birth date. [12]

Calculations for the birth date of Zoroaster have also been made based on the entire contents of the Avesta. For instance, various attempts have been made to calculate the date by analyzing the contents of the Gathas, even though the information they provide lacks concrete evidence. One line of inquiry, based on the linguistic antiquity and the socio-cultural allusions within the Gathas, puts the date of Zoroaster anywhere between 1500 and 1000 BCE. [13] Another line of inquiry, based on literary, historical, and theological evidence, puts the date of Zoroaster anywhere between 900 and 400 BCE. [14]

Again, a literary study of the Yashts (a section in the Avesta) resulted in proposing for Zoroaster's life span the dates 650 to 600 BCE. [15] An account of the Zoroastrian theory of world-ages in the Bundahishn (Zoroastrian religious documents) has led to a proposed date of 595 BCE for the founding of Zoroastrianism. [16] And an investigation of certain inscriptions related to the Achaemenid dynasty and the Zoroastrian religion sets Zoroaster's life span at 559 to 522 BCE. [17]

Thus, this brief survey clearly indicates one point: the available information for calculating Zoroaster's dates is quite conflicting. The birth dates derived by ancient Greek and Latin writers tax the scholar's credulity. The birth date suggested by al-Biruni is suspect, since it seems to derive from later, popular Iranian belief that is itself questionable. The arguments put forward through an analysis of various scriptural and inscriptional information are not sufficiently solidly based to be convincing. That leaves us with the linguistic characteristics of the Gathas. At first sight this type of analysis seems to offer the most reliable solution. And yet, one must recognize that there is a methodological difficulty. I do not believe that our information on language use and language development is anywhere near adequate to permit its use as a basis for dating. So, until something better is suggested, the tradition of placing Zoroaster at about the seventh to sixth centuries BCE may have to be allowed to stand.

Birthplace

The birth-place of Zoroaster is also a difficult matter to resolve. The two main possibilities are north-east and north-west Iran. The geographical allusions in the Avesta are of little help (e.g., Yasht 1, 10, 19; Videvdat 1, 19; cf. also Bundahishn 5, 20, 21, 29), and the language of the Gathas betrays both a north-western and a north-eastern dialect.[18] The dispute over these linguistic and territorial differences is sometimes reconciled by suggesting that Zoroaster was born in one area (either north-east or north-west Iran) and later lived and worked in the other area.[19]

Greek and Latin writers are also divided in their opinion as to the homeland of Zoroaster.[20] Some, such as Cephalion, Eusebius, and Justin, believe it is Bactria and the east. Others, such as Pliny and Origen, suggest Media and the west.

Islamic authors, such as Shahrastani (1086–1153) and at-Tabari (ca. 839–923), also imply that Zoroaster's birth-place is western Iran.[21] In fact, Arab sources, such as ibn-Hurdadhbah (ca. 816) and Yaqut (ca. 1220), specify the birth-place of Zoroaster to be the city of Urmiah (or Urmia, presently called Rizaijeh) in Shiz, a district of Azerbaijan.[22]

Because the reliability of classical writers and Islamic authors is open to question, and the information provided by the Avesta and the Gathas is of no great help, some scholars have gone as far as to doubt the historicity of Zoroaster.[23] But such an argument is unwarranted, because the evidence, even if it is conflicting, indisputably points to the contrary.[24] In spite of the painstaking research in the field of Zoroastrian (or Iranian) archaeology, ethnology, philology, religious literature, and history, there is still no consensus of opinion on Zoroaster's life. This, of course, is not surprising at all, because there is a confusing mixture of fact, legend, and myth in all the sources. The task of separating trustworthy Zoroastrian tradition from fanciful lore has been pursued by reputable scholars, but while there is a large measure of agreement among these scholars, the debate is still far from being over. Thus, since we lack precise biographical data, we must be satisfied for the moment to accept the following tentative conclusions.

Zoroaster was born in Iran at the end of the seventh or the beginning of the sixth century BCE, the period preceding the formation of the Persian empire under Cyrus II (559–529 BCE). He was trained to be a priest, since he refers to himself as a *zaotar*, the chief priest to officiate in the ritual of sacrifice.[25] Whether he chose his priestly function or acquired it through heredity is difficult to assess, although the former seems more likely. His father's name was Pourushaspa and his mother's Dughdova. He was married and had several children.

Furthermore, the Gathas indicate unmistakably the personal relationship – a passionate, intense dialogue – that Zoroaster had with his God, Ahura Mazda. His spiritual visions created in him a religious zeal to proselytize, but his initial efforts at spreading "the good religion" and winning support for his views met with hostility and failure. Eventually, however, Zoroaster found a patron, King Vishtaspa, who not only accepted Zoroaster's faith but helped propagate it throughout his kingdom.

Beyond these few facts, nothing more can be said with certainty about Zoroaster's life.

Teachings

What about the teachings of Zoroaster? In what way did the nature of his message differ from ancient Iranian beliefs and practices? Did his teaching represent an "apparent dualism" or an "imperfect monotheism"? Did he believe that the world was ruled by two opposing principles, one good and the other evil? Or did he insist on the supremacy of one God?

These questions have long been the subject of dispute, and once again the difficultly lies in the surviving literature, the inscriptional evidence, and the archaeological finds.[26] Nevertheless, it is possible to sketch the main lines of thought of Zoroaster within the context of ancient Iranian beliefs and practices. In fact, our knowledge is further enhanced by the affinities that exist between the Iranian and Indian (Vedic, Hindu) religious concepts and social customs.

There were several important Iranian divinities who were either ignored, condemned, or assumed by Zoroaster. These Iranian divinities were divided between the benevolent (*ahura*) and malevolent (*daeva*) deities (reversed in the Vedic pantheon, *asura* is malevolent and *deva* benevolent). The Iranian Mithra (IN Mitra), for instance, was the protector of those who were faithful to their contracts (i.e. covenants), and the enemy of those who betrayed their contracts (Yasht 10). He was the god of social order, uniting the different groups of society, and the god of justice. But he was also depicted as the god of fate, war, and victory. He was imagined to ride in a carriage drawn by white horses. Sacrifice and libation (*haoma*, IN *soma*) was important in his cult. His strongest rival was the deity Ahura Mazda.

Indra (IN Indra) was the god to whom people called when seeking victory in battle. But he was also the god who wreaked vengeance upon those who did not recognize the sacredness of contracts or treaties. The functions of Indra and Mithra seem essentially similar: both punished those who broke their contract treaty. But Mithra, in addition, protected those who were faithful.

Vayu, the god of wind, was probably in origin a malevolent deity, but later he was neatly bisected to become the good Vayu, who protected the creatures of Ahura Mazda, and the evil Vayu, who was little better than a demon of death (Yasht 15.5, 57). Anahita, the fertility goddess, was associated with water and a river, whose waters gave life and fertility to humans, animals, and plants (Yasht 5.2, 34, 120, 130). Her sacred animal was the beaver, and her cultic image was represented as a beautiful, radiant figure dressed in beaver fur.[27]

Vivahvant (IN Vivasvant), originally a sun god, established a rite in which the juice of the god-plant *haoma* (IN *soma*, a species of ephedra) was extracted or pressed and ritually consumed.[28] In return, he was granted a son whose name was Yima (IN Yama). Yima was responsible for the destiny of the human race (Yasna 9.4–5; Yasht 5.25–26, 15.15–16, 17.28–31, 19.36–38; Videvdat 2). Consequently a web of legends was woven around him, two of which prove the importance of this deity among the ancient Iranians.[29]

According to one legend, Yima had a golden reign of one thousand years during which he deprived the malevolent deities of their prosperity, and took away their power to inflict cold or heat, old age, death, or disease on their victims (Yasna 9.10, 17.30, 19.32–33). This golden age, however, did not last forever, because Yima sinned and human beings lost their immortality. Then the wise father, Vivahvant, warned Yima to retreat underground as humanity was to be afflicted by winter. There Yima was to remain, together with his followers, until the signs foreshadowing the last days appeared – the worst being a winter more terrible than any the world had ever seen. Then Yima was to re-emerge and re-populate the devastated earth.

According to another legend, Yima was the institutor of the bull-sacrifice, the ritualistic observance of which was believed to banish from the world disease, old age, and death. Those who consumed the flesh of the sacrifice given them by Yima became immortal (Yasna 32.8). That this sacrifice took place after dark, or in a sunless place, seems to be implied by Zoroaster's condemnation of those priests who said that the sun and the ox were the worst things the eye could see (Yasna 32.10). Moreover, this animal sacrifice, combined with the rite of *haoma*, must have been an unseemly and orgiastic affair accompanied by shouts of joy, because Zoroaster condemned the filthy (literally "urine") drunkenness of the priests, and their attempts to deceive the people (Yasna 48.10; cf. Herodotus 4.75). Whether Zoroaster was opposed to the ritual as such, or only to the form of the ritual, is difficult to decide. But the bull-sacrifice is still practised today in various forms (see Chapter Five).

Turning for comparison to ancient Iranian religious concepts, the first in importance was *asha*, meaning truth, or order. The principle that violated *asha* was *druj*, meaning falsehood, or disorder. Zoroaster, who seems to have adopted this basic duality, described himself as a true enemy of the followers of *druj* and a powerful supporter of the followers of *asha* (Yasna 43.8). These concepts of order and disorder, or truth and falsehood, belonged to the realm of nature as well as to that of cultic rites and moral law. Zoroaster asked his God to tell him who was "in the beginning the father to *asha*," to which Ahura Mazda replied that he "the Wise One was the father of *asha*" (Yasna 44.3, 47.2).

Thus, Zoroaster's religious innovation rests on his familiarity with ancient Iranian tradition and on his skill in rejecting or reformulating the beliefs and practices of that tradition. This, of course, does not belittle his achievement; on the contrary, it was quite radical, especially when seen against a polytheistic background. Indeed, the religious corruption of his day deeply offended him, particularly the base practices of the Iranian priests, who through their evil actions diverted people from the best course of action and the divine purpose in life (Yasna 32.9–12). Without doubt, such were the followers of *druj*, and Zoroaster openly condemned them as the beloved of the malevolent deities (*daeva*) and obstructors of the Good Mind, departing from the divine purpose of Ahura Mazda and from his law (Yasna 32.4, 11). That such a pronouncement would bring him into sharp conflict with the sacrificial priests he knew very well; yet in the face of persecution, he spoke courageously against them, calling them wilfully blind and deaf and accusing them of hindering the noble principles of truth and good thought through their own deceitful actions and doctrines (Yasna 51.4).

Against a pantheon of Iranian deities, some benevolent, others malevolent, Zoroaster upheld the supremacy of Ahura Mazda, the lord of life and wisdom, the first and last for all eternity (Yasna 31.8, 43.16). Moreover, Ahura Mazda was mighty and holy, the creator of all, giver of all good, and the giver of life (Yasna 43.4, 44.7, 48.3, 50.11). To those who looked up to Ahura Mazda with awe, to them he was a friend, brother, and father (Yasna 45.11). Because Ahura

Mazda was holy, eternal, just, omniscient, the primeval being, creator of all and the origin of all goodness, Zoroaster chose him as his sole God (Yasna 29.6, 43.4, 43.5, 45.3, 46.3). Thus, Zoroaster took over the ancient Iranian belief in the *ahura* (benevolent gods) and transferred that belief to a sole Ahura whom he saw as the Mazda (Wisdom), and who was therefore called Ahura Mazda, meaning Wise Lord.[30]

The relationship of Ahura Mazda to other divine powers or entities, known as Yazad (Yazata), described by Zoroaster is not easy to define. Ahura Mazda is spoken of as the father of Vohu Mana (Good Mind), as he is also the father of Asha (Truth), and his daughter is Aramaiti (Right Mind). But Ahura Mazda is also the true creator of Asha (Yasna 31.8, 44.3, 45.4, 47.1,2). Through the Spenta Mainyu (Good Spirit) and the Vohu Mana (Good Mind), Ahura Mazda grants Haurvatat (Perfection) and Ameretat (Immortality) to those whose words and deeds are in harmony with Asha (Truth), Xshathra (Kingdom, Majesty), and Aramaiti (Right Mind).

According to ancient Iranian belief, Ahura Mazda was the wise lord, the all-knowing sky god, and the supreme creator. He was also intimately associated with truth, sovereignty, mysterious power, light, and sun. His nature was best expressed in the cult of fire (*atar*). The ritual attached to the sacred fire existed before Zoroaster, who adopted it and made it the outward symbol of truth (Yasna 43.4, 9). In fact, Zoroaster taught that, for an individual to exercise free choice intelligently, Ahura Mazda gave his pure mind and his flaming fire of thought (Yasna 46.7). This fire was an enduring, blazing flame bringing clear guidance and joy to the true believer but destruction to lovers of evil (Yasna 34.4). It was through the energy of fire that Ahura Mazda assigned judgment to truth-followers and to evil-followers (Yasna 43.4, 47.6).

Zoroaster saw humanity divided into two opposing parties: the truth-followers (*ashavant*), who were just and god-fearing; and the evil-followers (*dregvant*), among whom were classed all evil rulers, evil-doers, evil-speakers, those of evil conscience, and evil-thinkers (Yasna 49.11). But this basic dualism that Zoroaster saw here and now on earth he projected to the whole cosmos. He came to see that this fundamental tension existed both in the material as well as in the spiritual spheres. Over against a transcendental good mind stood the evil mind; over against the good spirit stood the evil spirit; and so on. Yet, on every level, a choice had to be made. This insistence on freedom of choice was the marked characteristic of Zoroaster's teaching. In fact, what stood out in Zoroaster's principles was not the ethical dualism of good versus evil but the importance of the individual as an arbiter between them. Each individual was ultimately faced with making a choice between good and evil, truth and falsehood.

Zoroaster's concept of dualism and free choice seems to have derived from an ancient Iranian myth of "the two uncreated Mainyu" (Spirit/Being): Spenta Mainyu (Spenta = Good, Bounteous, Holy – the later Ahura Mazda) versus Angra Mainyu (Angra = Evil, Destructive – the later Ahriman).[31] The one, the bringer of life and abundance, was good in thought, speech, and deed; the other, the author of death and destruction, was evil in thought, speech, and deed. And human beings, Zoroaster said, could exercise their freedom to follow one of the two. This is expressed with characteristic force in the following words:

Listen with your ears to the best things. Reflect with a clear mind – man by man for himself – upon the two choices of decision, being aware to declare yourselves to Him before the great retribution [i.e., final judgment]. Yes, there are two fundamental spirits, twins which are renowned to be in conflict. In thought and in word, in action, they are two: the good and the bad. And between these two, the beneficent have chosen correctly, not so the maleficent. Furthermore, when these two spirits first came together, they created life and death, and how, at the end, the worst existence [i.e., hell] shall be for the deceitful, but the best thinking [i.e., Heaven] for the truthful person. (Yasna 30.2–4)[32]

Thus, side by side with the fundamental principle of freedom of choice, Zoroaster taught that the good was its own reward; that happiness and misery were the consequences of a man's good and evil deeds (Yasna 33.2–3). He saw the final consummation of creation, at which time Ahura Mazda was to come with his three powers; that ultimately sinners would deliver the evil/falsehood into the hands of truth; and that eternal joy would reign everywhere. This is best expressed in the following Gathic verses.

But I have already realized Thee to be virtuous, Wise Lord, when I saw Thee to be the First One at the creation of the world, and when I saw that Thou didst determine actions as well as words to have their prizes, namely, bad for the bad, a good reward for the good, (each to be given) through thy skill at the final turning point of creation. (Yasna 43.5)[33]

And thus, when the punishment for those sinners shall come to pass, then, for Thee, Wise One, shall the rule of good thinking be at hand, in order to be announced to those, Lord, who shall deliver deceit into the hands of truth. (Yasna 30.8)[34]

Moreover, the souls of humans were to be judged at the "bridge of the judge." The just would receive their eternal reward, while the wicked, their final doom. Again, this is graphically expressed in the following passages:

... the deceitful person misses the true (conception) of the honest man. His soul shall vex him at the Bridge of the Judge. (Yasna 51.57)[35]

Wise One, Thou dost guard in Thy house ... the souls of the truthful ones.... But the deceitful persons, bad in rule, bad in actions and words, bad in conceptions and thoughts, them shall their souls continue to encounter with foul food when they shall be the true guests in the House of Deceit [i.e., hell]. (Yasna 49.10–11)[36]

Hell was the abode of all evil rulers, evil-doers, evil-speakers, those of evil conscience, and evil-thinkers (Yasna 46.7, 46.11, 49.11, 51.14). Heaven was the abode of the righteous, who would be blessed with Ahura Mazda's reward of perfection and immortality (Yasna 31.21, 32.13, 32.15, 51.15). Humans assisted the cause of Ahura Mazda by choosing good deeds, good words, and good thoughts.

Deeply rooted in Zoroaster's teaching, then, was the moral responsibility of choice. This meant that each individual held the key to his or her own destiny by exercising his or her own choice between good and evil, truth and falsehood. But the cause of truth demanded the crushing of evil. Thus, the decision to follow truth necessarily implied a commitment to Ahura Mazda, the very essence of truth, both in the moral and physical order. And it is precisely here that Zoroaster called everyone to join in combat against the forces of evil in order to bring about the ultimate triumph of Ahura Mazda and of all the eternal forces of life.

This brings us to an important and controversial question: was Zoroaster a dualist or a monotheist? Four critical opinions have been proposed. First, some insist that Zoroaster was a dualist.[37] Second, others argue, just as forcefully and as satisfactorily, for the opposite: that Zoroaster was a monotheist.[38] Third, a number of scholars combine the two arguments by suggesting that Zoroaster was both a monotheist and a dualist.[39] And fourth, one scholar suggests that Zoroaster was neither a monotheist nor a dualist but a prophet who stands at an early stage in a continuum that is to be traced from mythology to philosophy.[40]

To recount the arguments put forward by various critics is tedious and unnecessary. Suffice it to say that the enigmatic nature of the sources permits the proliferation of differing views. Indeed, most of the information we possess seem to fluctuate between dualistic and monotheistic concepts.[41] A few instances will suffice to illustrate this problem.

First, Zoroaster's teachings imply that there is an inherent imbalance of power between the two separate primordial forces of good and evil. What is insisted upon in all the sacred texts is the total destruction of the evil principle by the good force; the complete and final triumph of Ahura Mazda to reign supreme; and the end of human history.

Second, the ideas of Zoroaster explain Ahura Mazda's claim to infinite wisdom. The unintelligent (virtually ignorant), deceitful machinations of the rival, evil principle are simply no match for Ahura Mazda's intelligence, forethought, and insight.

Third, Zoroaster's theory of human nature adequately justifies the critical role of human allegiance: the course of human history depends on the choice humans make. But humans possess a "natural responsiveness" to Ahura Mazda's persuasive power, which makes the evil principle's defeat inevitable. This means that human acts, words, and thoughts are decisive in shaping cosmic values.

What then may be concluded from all of this? It seems that Zoroaster tried to reform the ancient Iranian polytheistic concept by promoting the supremacy of Ahura Mazda.[42] With Ahura Mazda as the only god, the notions hitherto associated in the ancient Iranian cosmology with the other *ahura* and *daeva* became subordinate to him. And perhaps, without taking away all their primitive meaning, Zoroaster made these notions the powers or entities of Ahura Mazda. Furthermore, the elements of struggle that lay scattered in the ancient Iranian myths of gods, demons and monsters Zoroaster welded into a single universal conflict: good versus evil, in which God and humans took part together. To be sure, the evil principle co-existed with Ahura Mazda, but in no way was it co-equal, co-eternal, or even worthy of worship. In fact, the inevitable outcome was the destruction of the evil principle, the end of human history, the judgment of human beings, the reward and punishment of each individual, and the supreme reign of Ahura Mazda throughout eternity. In other words, Zoroaster's teachings imply that he perceived two distinct ages: this present, temporal, "dualistic age," to be followed by an eternal, "monotheistic age," thanks to the responsive choice of human beings.

CHAPTER TWO

Zoroastrian History

SPREAD OF ZOROASTER'S FAITH

Practically nothing is known of the way in which Zoroaster's faith spread through the Iranian lands during the Achaemenid dynasty.[1] Four principal sources of information are at our disposal: the Avesta, the Old Persian inscriptions, several archaeological finds, and some notices in classical writings.[2] These sources lack sufficient evidence for determining finally the official religion of the Achaemenids. Nonetheless, three different conclusions have been derived from the analysis of this evidence.

One view, which takes for granted the identity of Vishtaspa as the father of Darius and the protector of the prophet Zoroaster, holds that the Achaemenid kings were "true" Zoroastrians.[3] Another view diametrically opposes this theory and argues that the religion of the Achaemenids was identical with the ancient Indo-Iranian beliefs and views.[4] The third view attempts to combine the first two by proposing that the official state religion of the Achaemenids underwent two stages: (1) under Darius (552–486 BCE) the state embraced Zarathustrianism, the teachings of the prophet; (2) following Artaxerxes I (465–424 BCE) the state adopted Zoroastrianism, a mixed religion.[5]

Needless to say, each of these three views has some merit. The first view is based primarily on the evidence of the tradition in the Avesta. The second and third views are based on the Old Persian inscriptions, combined with some archaeological finds and the information supplied by classical writers, particularly the histories of Herodotus. Hence, an examination of the evidence can help us understand the difficulties inherent in tracing the development of Zoroaster's faith during the Achaemenid period.

The Old Persian inscriptions give evidence that three Achaemenid kings, Darius (522–486 BCE), Xerxes I (486–465 BCE), and Artaxerxes II (404–359 BCE), considered their god Ahura Mazda to be a great god, creator of all, and benefactor of every living creature, by whose help the kings accomplished their deeds.

Saith Darius the King: This which I did, in one and the same year, by the favour of Ahuramazda I did; Ahuramazda bore me aid, and the other gods who are ...

A great god is Ahuramazda, who created this earth, who created yonder sky, who created man, who created happiness for man, who made Darius king ...[6]

Saith Xerxes the King: ... among these countries there was [a place] where previously *daivas* were worshipped. Afterwards, by the favor of Ahuramazda, I destroyed that sanctuary of demons and I made proclamation, "The demons, shall not be worshipped!" Where previously the demons were worshipped, there I worshipped Ahuramazda and Arta ...[7]

Saith Artaxerxes the Great King: ... by the favour of Ahuramazda, Anaitis, and Mithras, this palace I built ...

A great god is Ahuramazda, the greatest of gods, who created this earth, who created yonder sky, who created man, who created happiness for man ...[8]

All three kings proclaim Ahura Mazda a great god, not the sole god. Artaxerxes tells us explicitly that Ahura Mazda is the greatest of gods, that is to say, the greatest among other gods. Furthermore, Artaxerxes speaks of the favour bestowed upon him not only by Ahura Mazda but also by two other deities, Anaitis and Mithras. Similarly, Darius clearly indicates that his success cannot be credited to Ahura Mazda alone but to other gods as well. Xerxes speaks of two deities, Ahura Mazda and Arta, and states that, where previously the demons had been worshipped, he established the worship of these two gods. Thus, these statements lead us to conclude that, while other gods were recognized, Zoroaster's teachings must have found receptive ears within the Achaemenid empire, as at least three kings mention the prophet's god in their inscriptions.

Another inscription alludes to the ethical dualism subscribed to by Darius. Here Darius's reference to other gods is unclear, but his statement with respect to his success is quite explicit:

Saith Darius the King: For this reason Ahuramazda bore aid, and the other gods who are, because I was not hostile, I was not Lie-follower, I was not a doer of wrong ...[9]

One is almost tempted to say that Darius boasted of not being a *dregvant* (follower of falsehood) but of being an *ashavant* (follower of truth). Whether Darius had this inscribed before his death, or whether the Zoroastrians, who may have had the upper hand by then, inscribed this after his death need not concern us. Suffice it to say that Darius's inscription suggests that the Achaemenids subscribed to the dualistic concept of "truth and falsehood" as taught by Zoroaster.

Another source of information is found in the writings of Herodotus. His observations concerning Achaemenid religion present a different picture. He states that the Persians offered sacrifices to the following gods: the whole circle of the sky called Zeus, the sun, the moon, earth, fire, water, and the winds (Herodotus 1.131–2). It is irrelevant whether Herodotus was right or wrong in his identification of names (Zeus, not Mitra) with regard to the sky and heavenly firmament. What is important is that the polytheistic pantheon that he describes corresponds to the Indo-Aryan legacy that the Achaemenids claimed as their heritage.

As a matter of fact, most of these Indo-Aryan gods may be identified. The sun god was Vivahvant, who had a son, Yima; both were responsible for the animal and drink sacrifices (Yasna 32.8, 9.10, 17.30, 19.32–33). Herodotus states that at sunrise Xerxes prayed to the sun god to let nothing happen that might prevent him from pursuing the conquest of Europe (Herodotus 7.54). The fire god was Atar, who was venerated by the Indo-Iranians from time immemorial, and who became supremely sacred in Zoroaster's doctrine (Yasna 43.4, 9). Again, in speaking of the impious act of Cambyses in Memphis, Egypt, Herodotus states that Cambyses's command to burn the embalmed body of Amasis was not only contrary to both Persian and Egyptian customs but a sacrilegious act, because "the Persians venerate fire as a god" (Herodotus 3.16). The Indo-Aryan wind god was Vayu, and Herodotus states that when the Persian fleet of Xerxes had encountered a great storm, they were able to calm it "by offering sacrifices and chanting spells to the wind" (Herodotus 7.191). The Indo-Aryan water god was Haurvatat, and we learn from Herodotus that the Persians "never make water nor spit into a river nor wash their hands in it ... for they have great reverence for the rivers" (Herodotus 1.138). This reverence for the water god is also seen in acts of Xerxes (religious or irreligious?), who is said to have scourged the Hellespont (Herodotus 7.35).

Thus, Herodotus does not seem to be aware of the proper Iranian names of gods, or of the benevolent and malevolent deities, let alone of Ahura Mazda. Furthermore, Herodotus does not show any knowledge of Indo-Iranian legends and myths, although he seems well versed in those of the Greeks. What he does observe, however, are the distinct religious customs and rituals of the Persians – that is, the external visible acts that can be observed by an outsider. And here, his observations are very interesting and may be considered under three headings: worship, sacrifice, and burial.

Worship

Herodotus states that the "Persians built no temples, no altars, made no images or statues" (Herodotus 1.131–2). From the Greek point of view he was probably correct; the Persians had no temples with altars and statues of the gods (as did the Babylonians and the Egyptians) where the faithful could worship. Nevertheless they did have fire-temples (altars), of which we know of at least two belonging to the Achaemenid period: one at Pasargadae built during Cyrus's reign (559–529 BCE), and the other at Naqs-i-Rustam in front of the tomb of Darius (522–486 BCE). [10] There is also a cylinder seal that depicts two priests standing in front of a fire-altar beneath the sacred image of Ahura Mazda, with a table upon which a mortar and pestle are displayed. [11] It appears, then, that the Persian religious ceremonies took place in the open air, for all the altars known to us – usually twin altars – have been found in the open country at some distance from the temples. [12] (One could also mention the Zendan-i-Suleiman building, but its function is by no means certain. [13])

Another valuable piece of information on Persian sanctuaries may be gathered from our evidence concerning the incident between Darius and the Magians. Our information on the Magians is very scanty. Their national and political aspirations may have revived for a short while when a certain Gaumata (GK Smerdis) attempted a coup during the reign of Cambyses. However, Darius's swift recovery of the empire from the Magians resulted in the recording of the following inscription:

Saith Darius the King: the kingdom which had been taken away from our family, that I put in its place; I re-established it on its foundation. As before, so I made the sanctuaries which Gaumata the Magian destroyed. [14]

Darius thus informs us that he restored not only the proper dynasty but also the sanctuaries destroyed by Gaumata the Magian.

These pieces of archaeological evidence lead us to conclude that, contrary to the statements made by Herodotus, the Persians had fire-temples, sanctuaries, altars, and images of divine beings. In fact, the winged figure of a divine essence in human form (speculated by scholars to be Ahura Mazda) is depicted, in addition to the cylinder seal, on the bas-reliefs above the royal Achaemenid tombs of Behistun, and on certain monuments at Persepolis.

Sacrifice

According to Herodotus, the custom of sacrifice among the Persians was as follows. He who offered sacrifice made no libation, nor used music, but went up to the highest mountain, leading the animal victim to a clean piece of ground, and invoked the god. This sacrifice was to be offered with the ministration of a Magian, who, at the end of the sacrifice, sang an ode concerning the origin of the gods (Herodotus 1.132). But Herodotus also states that, when Xerxes and his army came to the river Scamander, Xerxes went up to the citadel of Priam and there sacrificed a thousand oxen to Athene of Ilium, while the Magians poured libations to the heroes (Herodotus 7.43). And on another occasion, he states that Xerxes poured a libation into the sea from a golden cup (Herodotus 7.54).

What are we to make of the contradictory statements of Herodotus regarding the offering of libation? We know from the texts discovered in the archives at Persepolis that the Persian priests prepared an intoxicating drink (*haoma*) from a plant to be used for rituals, and the texts specify the profits made from its sale.[15] Further support comes from an actual mortar and pestle, used for *haoma*, found in Persepolis. Thus, the Persians must certainly have offered libations during their sacrificial offerings.

Burial

Herodotus's account clearly differentiates between the Persian and Magian customs of disposal of the dead (Herodotus 1.140). Unlike the Magians, who exposed the corpse to be torn by wild birds and beasts of prey, the Persians, states Herodotus, treated the corpse with wax and then covered it with earth. The Spring Cemetery of Persepolis and the Achaemenid rock-tombs present this evidence of Persian burial custom, as do the tombs of the Achaemenid kings at Pasargadae and Behistun.[16]

This brief survey of the Old Persian inscriptions, the statements of Herodotus, and the archaeological discoveries clearly indicates the difficulty of determining the religion of the Achaemenids. Nevertheless, several observations may be made based on an analysis of the evidence presented above.

The conflicting nature of our information does not permit us to argue convincingly that the Achaemenid kings embraced the "true" religion of Zoroaster. However much Darius's religious opinions seem to have approximated those of Zoroaster, and however zealous Xerxes may have been in his suppression of the cult of the *daevas*, the resurgence of other deities from the reign of Artaxerxes II onward proves that the ancient Indo-Aryan religious legacy continued to exist. Perhaps, during the two centuries of Achaemenid rule, the efforts of Zoroastrian adherents were directed to convert the kings in support of "the good religion." But there is no hard evidence of any active proselytizing.

It is quite possible that Zoroaster's religion found receptive ears among the Achaemenids. But side by side with the spread of Zoroastrianism there remained throughout the Achaemenid era the traditional Indo-Iranian pantheon and cult. In fact, our evidence indicates that at least three different forms of religion coexisted simultaneously in Achaemenid Persia: Zoroastrian, Magian, and Persian. Each inherited the religious legacy that belonged to the Indo-Aryan group, but in time each moulded its own distinct religious identity and pattern. And if that is the case, then we can say that Herodotus has no contradictory statements or accounts, but interestingly enough demonstrates how the Persians and the Magians (who both claimed the Indo-Aryan legacy) each preserved separate identities in the various phases of their religions.

Religion and politics went hand in hand in the ancient East, and therefore the differences between the two groups were reflected, although in a very subtle way, both in their religions and in their political spheres. Zoroaster, who was not welcome in his own country, had moved south-westward to the region where the Persians were established and whence they would soon emerge as great actors in the arena of world politics. If nothing else, his bringing of Ahura Mazda to the forefront was welcomed by the Achaemenid Persians. But side by side with the new Zoroastrian movement there remained the traditional pantheon and cult of the Persians and the Magians. Thus at least three religious forms – Zoroastrian, Magian, and Persian – coexisted in Achaemenid Persia.

SETBACK AND RECOVERY

The period of foreign domination of Persia by Alexander the Great and his successors, the Seleucids, following the Achaemenids, dealt a heavy blow to the development of the Zoroastrian community. Alexander's invasion and destruction was apparently so catastrophic that Alexander himself is depicted in Zoroastrian tradition as the *guzastag* (accursed), an epithet used to describe Ahriman (the Adversary), apostates, and opponents of the faith. Similarly, the material damage and moral crimes committed by Alexander and his cohorts are singled out in Zoroastrian tradition: temples and sanctuaries were plundered; priests who defended their holy places were slaughtered; and scriptures "written on oxhides with gold ink" were burned (Bundahishn 33.14; Denkard 5.3.14; Arda Wiraz Namag 1.1–11). Perhaps the greatest loss sustained by the Zoroastrians was in the death of their priests, who, as the "living books," handed down all tradition orally from one generation of priests to another. Nonetheless, much survived, and gradually the Zoroastrians regained their former strength, especially during the long reign of the Parthians.

The Parthians (247 BCE-226 CE) were a group of nomads who invaded and settled in Parthava (Parthia), in north-east Iran, some time during the third century BCE.[17] Soon they adopted the language, customs, and culture of their conquered subjects. In 247 BCE, Arshak (GK Arsaces, founder of the Arsacid dynasty) revolted against the Seleucids and gained the independence of Parthia.[18] From then on, all the successors of Arshak, comprising in all some thirty-nine kings, used his name as a title.[19] By the first century BCE the Arsacid dynasty (Parthian dynasty) had established their rule from the frontiers of India to the western borders of Mesopotamia (modern Iraq).

The Arsacid rulers set themselves up as heirs of the Achaemenids, adopted the old title "king of kings," transferred the seat of their rule to Ctesiphon, and made the Pahlavi language (Persian written in Aramaic characters) the official Parthian language.

Despite the damage suffered under Alexander the Great and his successors, the Zoroastrian faith, along with other forms of Iranian religion, flourished in the Parthian period. In fact, the Greek author Isidore of Charax, who lived close to the Persian Gulf around the end of the first century BCE, informs us that in the city of Asaak, where Arshak was proclaimed king, a "perpetual fire" existed, and that sacrifices were offered to Anahita at her temple in Ecbatana (modern Hamadan).[20] Other classical writers indicate the widespread worship of Mithra in the Parthian empire.[21] This is attested to by several prominent Arsacid monarchs, who honoured Mithra by assuming his name: Mithradates I (171–138/137 BCE), Mithradates II (123–88/87 BCE), Mithradates III (58/57–55 BCE), Mithradates IV (ca. 128–147 CE). Also, the hymn in praise of Mithra in the Zoroastrian scriptures (Yasht 10) is believed to date from the last years of the reign of Mithradates I.[22]

The spread of Zoroastrianism in the Parthian period may be deduced also from the Armenian sources.[23] These sources are of relatively late date (that is, from the Sasanid period, when Armenians embraced Christianity, in 301 CE) and written by Christian chroniclers who were partly hostile to their former Iranian religion. Nonetheless, the situation they describe was much the same as that of the Parthian period. These Armenian sources mention the following deities: Ahura Mazda (ARM Aramazd), as the head of the pantheon; Anahita (ARM Anahit) as the most favourite goddess; Verethraghna (ARM Vahagn) as the national god of war; as well as the sun, the moon, and other less popular deities. Ahura Mazda was worshipped as father of all deities, creator of heaven and earth, and bestower of all good things.[24] It is said, moreover, that sanctuaries of Ahura Mazda with perpetual fire-altars existed in various parts of Armenia, including the ancient city of Ani and in the village of Bagavand (Bagravand).[25] Also, the festival of Nao Roz (ARM Amanor or Navasard, meaning New Year) was celebrated in honour of Ahura Mazda.[26] Thus, the picture presented in these Armenian sources indicates the gradual spread of Zoroaster's faith during both the Achaemenid and Parthian period, though no exact knowledge may be obtained as to when or how.

Another interesting note is found in the Zoroastrian scriptures. The passage in question relates that King Valakhsh (Vologeses I, ca. 51–79 CE) was responsible for gathering and putting together the scattered remnants of the Zoroastrian scriptures destroyed by the ravages and devastation of Alexander and his cavalry (Denkard 4.24, 7.3).

To sum up, then, it appears that the religious milieu that emerged during the Parthian period offered no obstacles to Zoroastrianism. On the contrary, there seems to be a restoration, even a revival, of Zoroastrian ideas and practices.[27] To be sure, our knowledge of the religious situation during both the Achaemenid and Parthian regimes is far from complete. Nevertheless, the records do not indicate any religious conflict between adherents of Zoroastrian and non-Zoroastrian religions.

RELIGIOUS RIVALRY

A revolt, which began in the city of Istakhr in the Persian province of Fars (Persis) at the beginning of the third century CE, put an end to the empire of the Parthians. A certain Papak (son of the priest

Sasan, from whom the Sasanid dynasty possibly derives its name) seized power from the local governor in a *coup d'état*. Soon after, Papak died and Ardashir (OP Artaxser, perhaps the younger son of Papak) succeeded to his position. Unfortunately our source of information on the lineage of Ardashir is scanty and conflicting.[28] However, under Ardashir's leadership the rebellion against the long-established authority went swiftly. The fighting that inevitably broke out between Ardashir and the Parthian kings, Vologeses V (207–233 CE), Artabanus V (ca. 213–227 CE), and Artavasdes (ca. 227–229 CE), ended in victory for Ardashir, who now became master of the Persian empire.

The Sasanid empire (224–651 CE), which Ardashir founded, was engaged in constant conflict with the empire of the Romans. In particular, the hundred years of war between Rome and Persia, which began in 527, weakened both empires. Then, from the period of the death of Khosrow II in 628 to the end of the reign of the last Sasanid king, Yazdagird III, in 651, anarchy ensued, and various kings and pretenders followed one another. Yazdagird III was assassinated in 651 and the entire land of Iran fell to the Muslim Arab cohorts, who had penetrated into various parts of the Persian empire since 633. The victorious progress of the Arab conquerors was evidently so swift and so catastrophic that Zoroastrians to this day speak of "the ruin and devastation that came from the Arabs." Indeed, the Muslim Arab invasion in the seventh century destroyed the existing Persian (and Roman) political forces in the Middle East. Only a small territory in Turkey survived as the Byzantine empire, until it too was conquered by the Turks in 1453.

Under the Sasanid kings, Persia enjoyed a period of great cultural brilliance that endured until the advent of the Arabs. In fact, throughout most of their history the Sasanid kings continued consciously and vigorously to uphold the traditions of their Achaemenid predecessors. As a result, the Zoroastrian faith played a significant role in reviving national sentiment.

The first two Sasanid kings, Ardashir I (224–240) and Shapur I (240–272), are traditionally considered to be the founders of Mazdayasnian (worship of Mazda) orthodoxy (Denkard 3–4).[29] These two kings, it is said, continued the work of collecting the dispersed writings of the Zoroastrian scriptures that Valakhsh had begun (Denkard 4.25). Tradition also names a high priest, Tosar (or Tansar), as the artisan of reform and the principal agent for establishing Mazdayasnian orthodoxy as the state religion. But next to nothing is known about the religious measures undertaken by Tosar. Similarly, the little we know of the activities of the high priest

Karter (also written Kartir, Kirder) in organizing the religious hierarchy, in succeeding to destroy his great rival Mani, or in enforcing Mazdayasnian orthodoxy throughout the Persian empire hardly explains what constituted heresy or by what means orthodoxy was established. Clearly, the archaeological, epigraphical, and historical evidence put together would only, at best, give an outline of Zoroastrianism in the Sasanid era; it provides little, if any, information on the actual orthodox doctrines maintained by Zoroastrian thinkers, or on the religious controversies that plagued the empire.

Some of the evidence indicates that Zoroastrian orthodoxy required the elimination of all rival religious movements. Kartir, the chief organizer of Zoroastrian orthodoxy from the time of King Shapur I, left for posterity a remarkable inscription in which he boasts of the attacks conducted on the various religions in the empire, including Judaism, Christianity, Mazdakism, Manichaeism, Hinduism, and Buddhism.[30]

Indeed, a remarkable number of faiths, such as Manichaeism, Zurvanism, Mithraism, and the veneration of local deities such as Anahita and Ishtar, all enjoyed the strong support of the population. In addition, there were large Jewish colonies, actively propagating their faith since ancient times. Then, the slow but gradually growing religion of the Christians, with all its variations, was making converts among rich and poor. And within this diversity of religious faiths there existed a movement commonly called "gnosticism." The two most famous gnostic figures were Bardesanes and Marcion, both of whom are regarded as precursors of Mani, the founder of Manichaeism, and seem to have exerted important influence upon him.

Mani, the son of a Parthian nobleman, Patik, and his wife, Mariam, was born in Babylonia in 216 CE.[31] His father frequented, like so many of his day, the "house of idols," but shortly before Mani's birth he abandoned his former religion to join the sect "who practise ablutions." Nothing is known for certain about the "house of idols", though modern sources identify it variously as everything from a Syrian cult temple to a Buddhist shrine. Similarly, it is impossible to determine the sect that Patik joined, though here again speculations vary from some sort of ascetic group to the Mandaean (a Christian group) community.

The story goes that when Mani was twelve years old he received a divine revelation, which convinced him that he was chosen to preach a new faith. A second revelation occurred when Mani was twenty-four years old. An angel, it is recorded, appeared to him to tell him that the time had arrived to proclaim the message. In obedience to the angel's command, Mani proclaimed his revelation to his father and other senior members of his clan. Although they converted to his new faith, Mani's public preaching did not begin immediately in Persia. He first went to India (probably to the present territory of West Pakistan) where, most probably, he came into close contact with Buddhism, from which he seems to have adopted certain teachings and practices. In less than a year, Mani returned to Persia and soon succeeded in establishing good relations with the ruling Sasanid King Shapur. Apparently, when Mani presented King Shapur with his book *Shahbuhragan* (or *Book Dedicated to Shapur*), the king was so impressed by Mani's message that he agreed to let him preach throughout the Persian empire.

For the next thirty years, Mani's teaching spread rapidly, in spite of opposition from the various established religions. [32] Mani himself founded new communities wherever he travelled throughout the Persian empire. But he was not alone in spreading his faith, for he sent disciples all over, who seem to have been equally successful in winning converts. [33]

The teachings of Mani were most probably the result of a deliberate effort to adapt, and to adopt the principles of several faiths, including elements from the Zoroastrian, ancient Mesopotamian, Buddhist, and Christian religions. He took or discarded whatever he wished from other creeds. He was quite prepared to give to his predecessors, such as Buddha, Zoroaster, and Jesus, the credit they deserved. But he considered himself the promised "Paraclete" of Jesus, the seal of all previous prophets. He claimed to have ascended to heaven and there to have received the divine revelation in the form of a book, making him the sole possessor of absolute truth.

The details describing the arrest and death of Mani are difficult to interpret. It seems that the Zoroastrian priests, led by their chief priest, Kartir, were instrumental in the arrest and trial of Mani in 276, during the reign of King Bahram II, son of King Shapur. Following the instructions issued by King Bahram II, Mani presented himself to the royal residency, only to be met by a raging king and a stormy trial, ending with fetters locked upon his ankles, hands, and neck. Mani sensed that the end of his life was near and, therefore, spent the next twenty-six days talking to his most intimate disciples. Finally, sixty years old and weakened by fasting and mortification, Mani died. The news of his death spread rapidly throughout the whole city and people gathered in great crowds.

Whether or not he was flayed alive is not so clear. What seems more accurate is the report that the king ordered a burning torch to be thrust through his corpse before hanging his severed head over the city gate.

This change to a policy of opposition against adherents of differing religious faiths meant the destruction of various cult statues and the pillage of non-Zoroastrian religious buildings. Such religious measures seem to have been as much a part of Kartir's pious achievements as a policy of the Sasanid rulers. Gone was the tolerant attitude of the Parthians toward those who professed different faiths or observed different religious practices. Indeed, a statement in the Zoroastrian scriptures reveals a fascinating illustration of Sasanid religious policy. Shapur II (309–379) is said to have summoned individuals from all the regions of his empire for a disputation to inquire about true and false religions. After listening and examining their arguments, he concluded that the declaration as presented by Adurbad (perhaps his chief priest) was the true faith and that he would "not tolerate anyone of false religion" (Denkard 413.2–8). Acting on the instigation of his Zoroastrian chief priests, Shapur II in 322 launched an active persecution against those who "scorned the sun, despised the fire and did not honour the water."[34] Elsewhere it is said that a Persian high priest vindicated his interpretation of the Zoroastrian faith by undergoing, and surviving, the ancient ordeal of having molten metal poured on his chest. Unfortunately, nothing is said about the doctrines he upheld so valiantly, but it may be safely assumed that he was being tested for his heretical inclinations.

The confrontation of faiths continued intermittently throughout the entire Sasanid period. Certain Sasanid monarchs were kind to those observing alien religious traditions, allowing practices that must have seemed shocking to orthodox Zoroastrians. The magnanimity of Yazdagird I (339–421) in allowing Christians in his domain to bury their dead earned him in Zoroastrian circles the title of "the sinner," for he was breaking two fundamental Zoroastrian tenets: permitting burial of corpses, which pollute the good earth (as opposed to exposure on a tower to the sun and vultures), and showing kindness to infidels. His son Vahram V (or Varahran, 421–439), on the other hand, was a devout Zoroastrian who took stern measures against those who practised alien religious customs or disregarded the Zoroastrian observances. He also dragged out the dead who had been buried in the days of his father and scattered them under the sun.[35]

Punishments and persecutions were often provoked by the rash acts of the Christians themselves. Christians refused to observe the Zoroastrian purity laws. Christian priests destroyed as many fire-temples as they could or, instead, extinguished the sacred fire in the temple and celebrated mass.[36] Moreover, they characterized the Zoroastrians as "followers of the wicked Zardusht (Zoroaster), serving false gods and the natural elements."[37] And they refused to obey the king's command to stop recruiting, proselytizing, and converting the public.

Non-Zoroastrian sources (e.g., Armenian, Syriac, Greek, Arabic) provide further information, though, like the Zoroastrian sources, their reliability must always remain open to question. Armenian chroniclers, for instance, record the strict measures adopted by the Sasanid rulers.[38] Armenia, situated on the western borders of the Persian empire, was under Persian suzerainty for almost eight centuries, from about the sixth century BCE to the end of the third century CE. Throughout this entire period, and particularly during the latter part of the Parthian dynasty, Armenia was a predominantly Zoroastrian land.[39] In 301, less than a century after the establishment of the Sasanid dynasty, the vassal king of Armenia, Tiridates III, adopted the Christian religion and by royal edict proclaimed Christianity the official religion of Armenia. A few years later, the change of policy in favour of Christianity in the Roman Empire brought Armenia and Byzantium a little closer, a development that aggravated the growing power struggle, between Rome on the one hand and Persia on the other, over control of strategically important Armenia. The dispute was finally settled by partitioning Armenia in 387 CE. The major part fell under the suzerainty of Sasanid Persia. Now Armenia was torn between two factions: pro-Roman and pro-Persian.

This political division was compounded by a religious one, since the Christian religion was now associated with the power of Rome. Christian Armenians in Sasanid Persia inevitably became politically suspect in the eyes of the authorities. This gave rise to periodic religious persecution. Just as the Romans were promoting Christianity, the Sasanids were determined to establish Zoroastrianism throughout their empire. Consequently all sorts of tactics were used in pursuit of this goal.

Zoroastrian priests, according to the Armenian historian Yeghisheh, used all their political power to suppress, and even to exterminate, all non-Zoroastrian religions.[40] First, they incited King Yazdagird II (who ruled from 438–457) to abolish rival religions in favour of

Zoroastrianism. In the words of Yeghisheh, the Zoroastrian priests said to the king:

The gods who have granted you empire and victory over your enemies have no need of your worldly gifts. They simply request that you put an end to all human heresies and subject everyone to the Zoroastrian rules and faith.[41]

Next, the Zoroastrian priests launched an accusation against Christian Armenians, stating that they ignored the Zoroastrian gods, neglected to tend the fires pertaining to the fire-altars, and defiled the various elements considered to be sacred by the Zoroastrians. Here is the accusation according to Yeghisheh:

You have ignorantly gone astray from our true religion. You despise the gods, you extinguish the fire, you defile the water. By burying the dead under the earth you corrupt the earth, and by disobeying the ordinances of our religion you assist Ahriman.[42]

The persistent refusal of Armenians to abandon their Christian inclinations necessitated stricter measures. By royal proclamation, all non-Zoroastrian religions were to be abandoned, and everyone throughout the Sasanid empire was to adhere to the rules of the Zoroastrian priests. Again, according to Yeghisheh, the following royal edict was issued:

All peoples and tongues throughout my domain must abandon their false religions and must worship only the sun. They must sacrifice offerings to him and call him god. They must tend the fire. In addition to all of these, they must fulfill all the ordinances of the priests, without omitting any detail.[43]

Christian Armenians not only ignored this decree but attacked neighbouring towns, killed numerous Zoroastrian priests, devastated many fire-altars, and then seized the furniture and fixtures of the fire-altars and placed them in their churches. Naturally, the Zoroastrian priests retaliated, and within a short time these hostilities assumed enormous proportions, leading ultimately to the Armenian uprising on May 26, 451. From a military point of view, the Armenians were defeated. Moreover, the persecutions continued on and off for another thirty years until finally a treaty was signed at Noursag in 484 CE granting Armenians their religious freedom.

Undoubtedly, uprisings of various kinds were quite common in different parts of the Persian empire, and, from the Persian point of view, the Armenian revolt may have been considered an insurrection of no major consequence. However, opposition against Zoroastrian heresies and alien religious movements greatly strengthened during the reigns of Kavad (488–497; 499–531) and of his son and successor Khosrow I (531–579).

Kavad had inherited from his predecessor a country that was in a chaotic condition marked by war, oppression, economic disaster, social and political unrest, religious strife, and general discontent. He had to choose between the Zoroastrian priesthood and the powerful nobility on the one hand, and on the other a large group of Mazdakites who demanded far-reaching social reforms to improve their lot.[44] Kavad sided first with the Mazdakites, but the revolutionary reaction of both the aristocracy and the clergy forced him to withdraw his support.

The name of the Mazdakites is derived from that of its founder, Mazdak (son of Bamdad), about whom we know next to nothing except that he preached his religious and social doctrine at the end of the fifth century. Our knowledge about the Mazdakites is scanty, based on hostile records, and often unclear and contradictory in nature. Two persons, of whom we know little other than their names, are linked with the Mazdakites: Bundos, a Manichaean who lived for a time in Rome during the reign of Emperor Diocletian (245–313), and Zaradusht, a Zoroastrian priest in Fars in the fifth century. It is possible, though not certain, that these two men were the predecessors of Mazdak.

The teachings of Mazdak seem to include elements from many religious systems, including Gnosticism, Zoroastrianism, and Manichaeism, with a moral philosophy inspired by the principles of pacifism, abstinence, chastity, and equality. Mazdak believed that all existence or being is the result of divine dualism caused by a pure accident of the mixture (or separation) of two primordial principles, Light and Darkness. Moreover, he taught that there was a corresponding interaction between the spiritual macrocosm, the mesocosm (world), and the human microcosm. An individual could attain a redemptive knowledge by understanding the symbolic powers of letters, words, and numbers, and by realizing in himself the four powers (discernment, understanding, preservation, joy), which act through seven viziers circulating in twelve spiritual entities. The individual who possessed this inward secret or revelatory knowledge did not need to perform any more the outward religious observances.

Mazdak's greatest appeal, however, lay in his social theories, particularly the abolition of social inequalities. The universal cause of all strife and hatred, he asserted, was the desire for pleasure and material possessions. He stressed, therefore, the principles of social equality. Everything was to be shared as communal property, including wives and concubines. These "communistic" or "socialistic" ideas of abolishing personal possession and changing family structure were supported not only by the poor, peasants and slaves, but by King Kavad himself, who under the impact of Mazdak introduced a number of new laws related to Mazdakite ideas of social justice.

The reasons for the royal adoption of a system that had every chance of shaking the very bases of Iranian society are far from clear. Was it "royal opposition to the nobility and their power"?[45] Was it "the desolate state to which the empire had been reduced through invasions and other circumstances"?[46] Or was it "a reaction of the slaves, of the peasants who had become semi-slaves, and of the formerly free population of town and country against Feudalism and its 'enslaving' system, as a class struggle which was a protest against the harems of the nobility in which so many women were incarcerated"?[47] We simply do not know. What happened, however, is that Kavad's reform precipitated a revolution that caused him temporarily to lose his throne. The course of events leading to this conspiracy are unclear. It seems that both the rich and the Zoroastrian priesthood combined forces and succeeded in deposing and imprisoning Kavad. Two years later, in 499, Kavad escaped, and with the aid of the neighbouring Ephtalite army he regained his throne from his brother Jamasp.

After subduing some dissident tribes and concluding an agreement with Byzantium, Kavad decided to abandon the Mazdakites, who were instrumental in several uprisings involving expropriation of land, looting of property, and abductions of women. Hence, starting under Kavad's reign and continuing under his son and successor Khosrow I (Chosroes I), the Mazdakites met the same fate as the Manichaeans. Their leaders, including Mazdak, were overthrown and massacred, their books were burnt, and their goods confiscated. This, of course, crushed the Mazdakite movement as a sect, but its ideas persisted and spread for several centuries, right into Islamic times. Their name appears time and again as the common designation for social revolutionaries.

Khosrow I restored the old order. His religious conviction, his energetic support of the establishment of state religion, and his harsh measures to curb false religious movements assured him an honoured place in Zoroastrian tradition, even though late in his reign he displayed a relatively lenient spirit (Denkard 413.9–414.6). His son Hormizd IV (579–590), however, adopted a more tolerant attitude toward his infidel subjects. When the Zoroastrian priests urged him to force the rebels to obey the religious laws of the land, his answer was: "Cease to harass the Christians and exert yourselves diligently in doing good works, so that the Christians and the adherents of other religions seeing that may praise you for it and feel themselves drawn to our religion."[48]

These religious rivalries were hardly known to the Zoroastrians before the Sasanid period. Perhaps they were periodic and localized incidents that did not affect seriously the expansion of Zoroastrianism. Whatever the case may be, it appears that there never was a real religious unity, even under the most orthodox kings. Sacred fire-altars were established in numerous places throughout the land, and many acts of worship were performed at these sanctuaries. Liturgical and calendar reforms were instituted. Religious observances and rules of conduct related to various daily activities were carefully performed. The Avesta was faithfully recorded and canonized, though it is impossible to know how much was excluded or conflated. Matters pertaining to religious law were interpreted and administered by Zoroastrian priests. And there is no doubt that Zoroastrianism, with its major sanctuaries and its elaborate rites and observances, remained as the dominant religious force throughout the Sasanid period, commanding the allegiance of hundreds of thousands of adherents.

In the end, internal strife, assassinations, and rebellions by claimants and counter-claimants plagued the Sasanid throne. And yet, the greatest blow to Zoroastrianism came not from the internal disorder of their empire but from the Arab conquest of Persia. Driven by their newly adopted religious fervour and by their craving for power and wealth, the Muslim Arabs became masters of most of Persia. Whatever the reasons for the collapse of the Persian empire, the disappearance of the Sasanid rule deprived Zoroastrianism of the support it once enjoyed.

SURVIVAL THROUGH THE CENTURIES

In 651 the last Sasanid king, Yazdagird III, was assassinated, and the entire kingdom controlled by Persia fell without much resistance to the Muslim Arabs. Not much is known of the decline of Zoroastrianism under Islamic rule, nor of the degree to which the state religion of the Sasanid empire held sway and persisted with the advent of Islam. Doubtless, many adherents embraced Islam, either by conversion or by coercion. Whatever the case, the Muslim invasion not only arrested the expansion of Zoroastrianism but threatened to annihilate its adherents. The fate of Zoroastrians might well have been that of the Sumerians, Babylonians, Assyrians, Hittites, Hurrians, Canaanites, Arameans, and Egyptians. Through some unexplained course of events, however, a small group managed to survive the sweeping wave of the Muslim empire.

The lack of evidence makes the subsequent history of Zoroastrianism almost as difficult to trace as its early beginnings. From time to time Zoroastrians in Iran rose in rebellion, only to invite the persecution of the Muslims. Zoroastrian tradition speaks of "the ruin and devastation that comes from the Arabs," but how and why such disasters occurred is not exactly known. Somehow a minority group of Zoroastrians, identified by Muslims as *gabars* (infidels), have survived up to the present day in Iran.[49] Another small group of Zoroastrians left Iran in the eighth and ninth centuries to seek asylum in India, where, as descendants and survivors of the ancient Persians, or Parsees, they remain to this day. These Parsee emigrants, however, were not the first Persians on Indian soil. Many had settled in India even earlier, attracted by long-standing, close trade relations between the two countries, and as participants in successive military expeditions to Punjab and Sindh led by Sasanid kings. But there is very little, if any, accurate information about these early settlers, and one may assume that they were eventually integrated into Indian society.

Thus, the Zoroastrians that live in India today are the descendants of the refugees who fled Persia sometime after the Islamic conquest. It is these Parsees who are considered to be the founders of the modern Zoroastrian community in India. Unfortunately, nothing is known for certain about the circumstances or the stages of this migration of Zoroastrians from Persia. There are no documents dating earlier than 1600 that describe the exodus.[50]

The Persian national epic *Shah-nama*, written by Firdausi in the tenth century, tells only of the historical genesis and development of the Persian nation, starting from mythical antiquity and continuing up to the end of the Sasanid era.[51] There are reports written on the Parsees by European travellers to India from the fourteenth to the seventeenth centuries, but they are limited to comments on the social and religious differences between Parsees and Hindus.[52] The *Rivayats*, a collection of twenty-six letters exchanged between Persian and Indian Zoroastrian priests during the fifteenth to eighteenth centuries, consist mainly of instructions and advice on matters of religion.[53]

Thus, the only chronicle describing the exodus of the Zoroastrians from Persia is the *Quissa-i Sanjan*, written in Persian in 1600 at Nausari by the Zoroastrian priest Behman Kaikobad Sanjana.[54] However, the date of this document – some eight hundred years after the events it records – makes the reliability of its contents suspect, especially in regard to its chronology. Also lacking is a proper investigation or critical analysis of the chronicled events. Opinions of modern critics vary from "extremely informative" to "a palpable falsehood." No doubt the document is based on oral history, but it is difficult to distinguish legendary from historical events in the narrative because there are no other sources by which to verify its contents. Unsatisfactory as it may be, the *Quissa-i Sanjan* remains the scholar's chief resource in tracing the events that culminated in the arrival of the Zoroastrians in India.

According to this chronicle, those Zoroastrians who clung tenaciously to their religion were forced by the religious persecution of the Muslims to leave Persia and flee, first to the remote mountainous region of Khorasan. To what extent the Zoroastrians were subjected to "bloody suppression by fire and sword"[55] is disputable. At any rate, according to the *Quissa-i Sanjan*, the Zoroastrians who first sought refuge in Khorasan remained there for a hundred years before moving to Hormuz on the Persian Gulf. Fifteen years later they left Hormuz and sailed in "seven ships" to India, landing at Diu or Gujerat. Another nineteen years passed before a Hindu raja, Jadi Rana, gave the Zoroastrians refuge in Sanjan.

Needless to say, this story has been the subject of endless controversy. Disputed issues relate to the reasons that compelled Zoroastrians to leave Persia; the number of refugees who fled; the exact year of migration to India; the number of migrations; the first site of settlement in India; and the historical authenticity of Jadi Rana.[56] This is not the place to examine the relative merits of the arguments and controversies surrounding these issues. Suffice it to say that conflicting and inconsistent statements in the chronicle represent the main source of contention.

There is a more relevant reference in the *Quissa-i Sanjan* that deserves brief mention: it is a reference to the process by which Zoroastrians adapted to their new habitat after their arrival in India. The story, according to the chronicle, is that Jadi Rana, the Hindu ruler of Sanjan, imposed five conditions prior to granting the settlers refuge in his land. First, he required an explanation of the Zoroastrian religion. Second, the abandonment of the Persian mother tongue and the adoption of the Indian language. Third, the substitution of Indian for Persian female clothing. Fourth, the surrender of all weapons carried by males. And fifth, the conduct of all wedding ceremonies under the cover of darkness.

Whether or not this story has any factual basis, subsequent events attest that Zoroastrians have adapted in this way to their Indian environment. Gujerati has become the native language of the Zoroastrian community, while the sari is accepted as the traditional garment of Zoroastrian women. The remaining conditions are honoured in terms of the loyalty of Zoroastrians towards their respective governments and the temperate conduct they have consistently demonstrated in Zoroastrian religious rites and customs.

The arrival of the British in Bombay in the seventeenth century served to relieve the isolation of the Zoroastrian people following their unique, non-Hindu religious tradition in India. Here, in the midst of a predominantly eastern tradition, lived a group of people who for over seven centuries had retained their identity as Parsees.[57] The racial and religious characteristics that defied absorbtion or assimilation by the Hindu mainstream placed Zoroastrians in a very significant position. For the next few centuries they played an important role as mediators between the western powers, especially the British, and Indian society. Placed in a privileged position by virtue of their role as mediators, Zoroastrians were able to travel and settle in the West, particularly England.[58]

In search of more challenging opportunities and better conditions, numerous Zoroastrians have settled in various parts of the western hemisphere. Their contact with western civilization has made them victims as well as beneficiaries of westernization, industrialization, and technology. Consequently, their cultural customs and religious traditions have been dramatically changed.

The circumstances under which Zoroastrians left India and Iran to settle in the western world bear little comparison with their earlier flight from Iran to India. No religious persecution drove the Zoroastrians out of India, as it had earlier generations. True, the migration of Zoroastrians to the West, particularly in the last four decades or so, was motivated by threats, real or perceived; the treatment of religious minorities after India's independence in 1949 and Iran's Islamic revolution in 1979 were factors in the migration. But the emigrants to the western world did not seek refuge or asylum in a foreign territory as their ancestors had done; they came of their own choice to a welcoming country. The refugees from Iran to India were, by modern standards, uneducated, poor, and inept. It is not known how long it took before they adapted to their Indian environment, language, clothing, food, and customs. The emigrants to the West, however, are professionals, businessmen, well-to-do, and versatile. Their contact with western civilization in India prior to their arrival in the West prepared them for an easy transition to the culture and customs of their adopted homeland.

Today, adherents of the Zoroastrian faith still live in their ancient homeland in modern Iran, along the west coast of India, and in almost every major city in the West. The implication of this territorial distribution is quite obvious. Each Zoroastrian community exists in a predominantly religious society: Muslim Iran, Hindu India, and the Christian West. Any future study of Zoroastrian history must certainly take into account the dynamic societal forces in all these three areas that threaten or challenge the survival of the Zoroastrian tradition.

CHAPTER THREE

Zoroastrian Scriptures

AVESTA

To study the Zoroastrian faith simply as a compilation of facts, figures, and historical data is like examining fossils or pressed flowers – they lack life and reality. The vital aspect of Zoroastrianism is the vibrating pulse of faith, conviction, and commitment experienced by its followers. This experience is based partly on the growth of tradition and partly on the belief that a group of writings is divinely inspired, received directly from God. Thousands of Zoroastrian devotees, therefore, find comfort, guidance, and inspiration in the words recorded in their sacred scripture, the Avesta.[1]

Before presenting a brief description of the contents of the Avesta, it is important to know when and how the Avesta became established in the written form. The intention in raising these issues is neither to fix its date of composition, which is largely a matter for speculation, nor to examine the scholarly theories related to its recording, which are still unresolved.[2] Rather, it is to present a historical sketch of its fate through the centuries up to the present day.

History of the Avesta

In its present form, the Avesta (a word of uncertain meaning and derivation) is only a small remnant of a sacred literature of considerable extent. This may be deduced from the fragmentary character of the Avesta as now extant, and from the references in the surviving Zoroastrian literature (e.g., Denkard, Rivayats), which give a detailed account of the loss of the original Avestan writings during the dark centuries following the conquest of Alexander the Great. According to these traditional accounts, the twenty-one *nasks* (books, volumes) of the original Zoroastrian scriptures were somewhat encyclopaedic in character. Under the Achaemenid rulers, these books were deposited and preserved with great care in the royal treasuries of both Persepolis and Samarkand. According to tradition, these two archetype copies were destroyed during the invasion of Alexander in 330 BCE, when he burned the Achaemenid palace in Persepolis and when his conquering hordes plundered Samarkand.

The incursion of Alexander, followed by the Seleucid and Arsacid (Parthian) rulers in the next five centuries, ushered in a period of darkness in the history of the Zoroastrian scriptures. Perhaps, considerable portions of the texts were preserved in scattered works and in the memory of Zoroastrian priests. According to tradition, King Valakhsh (generally identified with the Arsacid King Vologese I, ca. 51–79 CE) ordered the search for and collection of all parts of the scriptures that had survived the ravages of time and insisted on the writing of such portions that were preserved in oral tradition. This work was then continued by two Sasanid kings, Artakhshir Papakan (226–240 CE, who commissioned the high priest Tansar to collect all the scattered fragments) and his son King Shahpur I (241–272 CE). A final revision of the Avesta was made during the reign of the Sasanid King Shahpur II (309–380 CE), at which time a "canonical" text, consisting of a fixed number of books, was established.

These traditional accounts raise several important questions. How reliable are the accounts regarding the recovery and recording of the Zoroastrian scriptures? Do these stories contain an element of political propaganda? In what language(s) was (were) the original text(s) written? These questions, among others, are matters of scholarly dispute, and no satisfactory conclusion has been reached yet.

The Arab conquest of Iran in the seventh century caused far more serious damage to the Zoroastrian scriptures than either the ravages of Alexander or the neglect of the Zoroastrian priests in the succeeding centuries. Civil disturbances, religious persecutions, and the burning of many Zoroastrian scriptures and books by the conquering Muslim Arabs forced the followers of Zoroaster to either abandon their faith or go into exile. A small group of Zoroastrians, who either remained in Iran or escaped to India, were able to preserve a small body of texts. These texts (or manuscripts) were recopied from time to time and constitute the Avesta in its present form. The oldest manuscripts preserved by the Zoroastrians in India date from the thirteenth century of this era, while those preserved by surviving Zoroastrians in Iran are from a later date, about the seventeenth century.

Thus, the surviving parts of the Avesta correspond little with the original twenty-one *nasks*, either in arrangement or in extent. Only two of the twenty-one *nasks* are considered to represent any degree of completeness: the Videvdat and the Stot-Yasht. The remaining parts show evidence of having been patched up and pieced together.

The dates of composition of the different parts of the surviving Avesta cannot easily be determined. The general view holds that the Gathas (a section within the Yasna) represent the oldest part, in substance as well as in form, dating back to an early period of the Zoroastrian tradition, possibly as early as the period of Zoroaster. Other parts of the Avesta, however, suggest a period as late as the time of the Sasanid kings. Based on the linguistic evidence of the Avesta, the extreme limits of the period of development would then be from the seventh century BCE (or earlier, depending on the dates of Zoroaster) to the fifth century CE.

The preservation of the extant parts of the Avesta was determined, it seems, by liturgical interests. Generally, the Avestan texts were used (and still are) in ritual observances and ceremonies. These liturgical scriptures must have been considered of such importance that they were cherished, preserved with great care, and copied over and over again. Those parts that possibly escaped destruction but were not used in ritual may have gradually fallen into disuse, resulting in the neglect of copying and their final disappearance. Thus, the selection of texts that has survived in the Avesta represents only a small part of the original Zoroastrian scriptures.

Contents of the Avesta

The Avesta consists of hymns, formulas, narratives, and laws, all composed and written over a long period of time. Two principal parts can be distinguished within the whole. The first part contains the Yasna (which includes the Gathas), the Visparad (or Vispared, Visprat), and the Videvdat (or Vendidad). The second part includes the Khordeh Avesta and the Yashts.

The Avesta is not as easy to read as the Bible or the Qur'an, but one can at least get an idea of its contents from a brief description of its parts and a summary of the chapters contained therein.

Yasna

The chief liturgy of the Zoroastrians is the Yasna, a term that literally means "sacrifice" (corresponding to the Sanskrit term *yajna*), and includes confession, invocation, prayer, exhortation, praise, worship, adoration, and offerings. Much of modern Zoroastrianism consists of intricate ritual and symbolic ceremonies meant to lead worshippers to a contemplation of Ahura Mazda and his divine powers and bounteous creation.

The Yasna is comprised of six Gathas (hymns or songs), plus a collection of formulas for prayer and liturgy. The Yasna as a whole is divided into seventy-two chapters. Linguistically, a distinction is made between the language of the Gathas and the rest of the Avesta.[3] The former is known as "Gathic language" because it is of a more ancient character; the latter is known as "Younger Avestan," or simply "Avestan." The linguistic and historical affinity between the Gathas and the Rig Vedas (the collection of sacred texts of ancient India, and the oldest known documents in Sanskrit) is so marked that the assumption of a common cultural and linguistic origin is generally accepted by scholars.

Five of the six Gathas (comprising the following seventeen chapters of the Yasna: 28–34, 43–51, 53) are generally considered to be the work of Zoroaster himself, though there is no agreement on what he composed. Some argue that Zoroaster himself composed the entire Gathas; others think that the Gathas were composed in the main by him, but occasional verses were later added by his disciples; still others suggest that the Gathas, although composed by Zoroaster, were preserved by memory for centuries before being written down (the weight of the evidence supports this). As to the sixth Gatha, this is not ascribed to Zoroaster because its content differs theologically from the rest, even though it is written in the same dialect as the other Gathas.

The order in which the Gathas were composed and their logical arrangement within the Avesta are problematic matters yet to be solved.

The six Gathas make up the following chapters of the Yasna:

Yasna 28–34   =   Ahunavaiti Gatha
Yasna 35–41   =   Haptanhaiti Gatha
Yasna 43–46   =   Ushtavaiti Gatha
Yasna 47–50   =   Spenta Mainyu Gatha
Yasna 51   =   Vohu Xshathra Gatha
Yasna 53   =   Vahishtoishti Gatha

An analysis of their contents shows that they concern themselves with diverse themes: the nature of Ahura Mazda and his divine powers or entities; the creation of the universe, including human beings; the origin of evil; the salvation and regeneration of the individual; a last judgment; future rewards and punishments; practical precepts for good conduct and behaviour; the intimate, almost ecstatic union of the human soul with God, and so on.

To summarize, what follows is an outline of the Yasna as a whole, chapter by chapter.

Yasna 1–8: these are prayers dedicated to the sacrificial offerings of bread, water, and milk.

Yasna 9–11: these chapters are hymns of praise addressed to *haoma.* In the first part, there is an imaginary dialogue between Zoroaster and *haoma* personified, in which Zoroaster seeks to find out who were the first four mortals to have prepared and offered the sacrifice of *haoma* and how they were rewarded for performing such a virtuous act. The remaining part consists of praises, in a series of prayers, addressed to the power of *haoma,* with a threat of curses upon all those who neglect the proper sacrificial offering of *haoma.*

Yasna 12–13: these chapters contain the Zoroastrian profession of faith. First the faithful must denounce the demons; next they must proclaim themselves worshippers of Ahura Mazda; they then affirm that they are adherents of Zoroaster; and finally they must exalt the worldly rulers/lords (*ratus*) of the different social strata.

Yasna 14–18: here are found invocations addressed to Ahura Mazda, to the Amesha Spenta, and to the different kinds of fire (*atar*). In essence, these chapters constitute a fresh beginning, similar to the chapters in Yasna 1–8.

Yasna 19–26 may be divided into two distinct parts: a commentary (and eulogy) on the three principal Zoroastrian prayers found in Yasna 27; and a sequence of invocations addressed to the sacrifice.

Yasna 27 contains the three principal Zoroastrian prayers, plus an additional prayer, repeated in Yasna 54.

Yasna 28–34, 43–50, 51, 53: these chapters are considered to be the source of information on Zoroaster and his teachings, written in an obscure Gathic dialect.

Yasna 35–41, 42, 52: these chapters contain prayers and invocations addressed to Ahura Mazda, to the Amesha Spenta, to the waters, to fire, and to the entire creation of clean or holy elements.

Yasna 54 contains the fourth prayer, found earlier in Yasna 27.

Yasna 55 is a eulogy on the texts of the Gathas and a group of other texts that are difficult to identify.

Yasna 56–72: here are found numerous prayers, blessings, invocations, and eulogies, addressed to Ahura Mazda, to the Amesha Spenta, and to the various divine beings, of which Yasna 71 is supposed to contain a complete list.

The importance of the Yasna in the daily life of Zoroastrians can hardly be stressed too strongly. In fact, the Gathas are considered to be the most precious possession belonging to Zoroastrians today. Besides being loved and revered by all devout followers, the Avesta is taught to the young, and its teachings form the basis of all philanthropists. Most Zoroastrians turn instinctively to it for spiritual consolation, particularly at times of difficulty and sorrow. Others study the Gathas in order to emulate the "good life" as Zoroaster proclaimed it. Like Zoroaster, their prophet, they desire to reach Ahura Mazda in fullness of knowledge through Vohu Mana (Good Mind) and yearn to receive the blessings that come from following Asha (Truth or Righteousness). The following selections from the Yasna and the Gathas of Zoroaster will give a general sense of the importance of prayer and devotion to Ahura Mazda and his divine powers and bounteous creation.[4]

Yasna 1

1. I announce and I (will) complete (my worship) to Ahura Mazda, the creator, the radiant and glorious, the greatest and the best, the most beautiful, the most firm, the wisest, and the one of all whose body is the most perfect, who attains His ends the most infallibly, because of His Righteous Order, to Him who disposes our minds aright, who sends His joy-creating grace afar; who made us, and has fashioned us, and who has nourished and protected us, who is the most bounteous Spirit!

2. I announce and I (will) complete (my worship) to the Good Mind (Vohu Manah), and to Righteousness the Best (Asha Vahishta), and to the Sovereignty which is to be desired (Khshathra Vairya), and to Piety the Bountiful (Spenta Armaiti), and to the two, the Universal Weal (Haurvatat) and Immortality (Ameretat)...

11. And I announce and I complete (my worship) to all the stars. ... to the Moon ... to the resplendent Sun ... to Ahura Mazda ... to the Fravashis of the saints ...

12. And I announce and complete my worship to thee, the Fire, O Ahura Mazda's son! together with all the fires, and to the good waters, even to all the waters made by Mazda, and to all the plants which Mazda made.

22. Yea, all ye lords, the greatest one, holy lords of the ritual order, if I have offended you by thought, or word or deed, whether with my will, or without intending error, I praise you (now the more) for this.

Yasna 2

2. ... I desire to approach Ahura Mazda with my praise, the holy lord of the ritual order, and the Bountiful Immortals (Amesha Spenta), all those who rule aright, and who dispose of all right, these also I desire to approach and with my praise.

11. ... I desire to approach Ahura and Mithra with my praise ... and the stars, moon, and sun with the Baresman plants ... and the good, heroic, bountiful Fravashis of the saints ...

13. ... yea, I desire to approach the Zarathustrian law with my praise, and (with it) its long descent, and the good Mazdayasnian Religion (as complete).

Yasna 31

5. Speak Thou, in order for me to discern that very good thing which has been created for me by truth, in order for me to know and to bear in mind with good thinking (that thing) of which I am to be the seer. Even those things, Wise Lord, which either shall not be or shall be.

8. Yes, although Thou are the First One, I realized Thee to be (ever) young in mind, Wise One, when I grasped Thee in a vision to be the Father of good thinking, the real Creator of truth, (and) the Lord of existence in Thy actions.

Yasna 43

4. Yes, I shall (truly) realize Thee to be both brave and virtuous, Wise One, if Thou shalt help me (now) with the very hand with which Thou dost hold those rewards Thou shalt give, through the heat of Thy truth-strong fire, to the deceitful and to the truthful....

14. Yes, Wise One, (grant) to me Thy proper support, which an able man, possessing such, should give to his friend and which has been obtained through Thy rule that is in accord with truth ...

Yasna 65

1. I will praise the water Ardvi Sura Anahita, the wide-flowing and healing in its influence, efficacious against the Daevas, devoted to Ahura's lore, and to be worshipped with sacrifice within the corporeal world, furthering all living things, and holy, helping on the increase and improvement of our herds and settlements, holy and increasing our wealth, holy, and helping on the progress of the Province ...

2. (Ardvi Sura Anahita) who purifies the seed of all male beings, who sanctifies the wombs of all women to the birth, who makes all women fortunate in labour, who brings all women a regular and timely flow of milk.

Yasna 71

2. ... We worship Ahura Mazda with our sacrifice (as) the holy lord of the ritual order; and we sacrifice to Zarathustra likewise as to a holy lord of the ritual order; and we sacrifice also to the Fravashi of Zarathustra ... And we sacrifice to the Bountiful Immortals (Amesha Spenta) of the saints.

5. And we worship the entire bounteous Mithra.... And we sacrifice to all the holy Yazads, heavenly and earthly; and we worship all the good, heroic, and bountiful Fravashis of the saints.

6. And we worship all the holy creatures which Mazda created ... And we worship all the five Gathas, the holy ones, and the entire Yasna.

Visparad

Analogous to the Yasna but supplementing it is a shorter liturgy called the Visparad, meaning "to all the lords, or divine beings." The Visparad is divided into twenty-three chapters (twenty-four or twenty-seven, according to some) and consists of additional invocations, praise, and offerings of homage to: Ahura Mazda; other divine beings; heads of spiritual and terrestrial worlds; all the lords in the water, the sky, and the entire animal kingdom (of the good creation only); and the six chiefs of the year (i.e., the six seasonal festivals, now called *gahambars*). These seasonal festivals are strictly observed by modern Zoroastrians because they are believed to have been instituted by Ahura Mazda in commemoration of the six periods during which the world was created. Hence, the prayers and invocations included in the Visparad are used especially during the celebration of the *gahambars*. The following selections reflect the recitations of prayers made by Zoroastrian priests during the ceremony.[5]

Visparad 5

1. I come to You, O Ye Bountiful Immortals! as a praiser priest, and invoker, as a memorizer, reciting (Your ritual), and as a chanter for Your sacrifice and homage, Your propitiation, and Your praise ...

2. And I make my offering to You, O Ye Bountiful Immortals, who rule aright, and who dispose (of all) aright! (Yea), I offer You the flesh of my body, and all the blessings of my life as well.

3. And I confess my belief in Thee, O Ahura Mazda! and as a Mazdayasnian of the order of Zarathustra, and in accordance with his Faith.

Visparad 15

1. Hold your feet in readiness, and your two hands, and your under-

standings, O ye Zarathustrian Mazdayasnians! for the well-doing of lawful deeds in accordance with the sacred Order, and for the avoidance of the unlawful and evil deeds which are contrary to the ritual.

Visparad 23

1. We worship Ahura Mazda as the best (worship to be offered in our gifts). We worship the Amesha Spenta (once more, and as) the best. We worship Asha Vahista (who is Righteousness the Best). And we sacrifice to those (prayers) which are evident as the best; that is the Praises of the Yasnas.... And we worship Heaven, which is the best world of the saints, bright and all-glorious; and we sacrifice likewise to the best approach which leads to it.

2. And we sacrifice to that reward, health, healing, furtherance, and increase, and to that victory which is within the two [prayers], Ahuna-vairya and the Airyema-ishyo, through the memorized recital of the good thoughts, words, and deeds (which they enjoin).

Videvdat

The Videvdat (or Vendidad, an abbreviated form of vi-daevo-datem, meaning "anti-demonic law" or "law abjuring demons") consists of twenty-two sections, called fargards.[6] Its date cannot be stated with certainty, but internal evidence suggests that "they were compiled, partly from older material, during the Parthian period."[7]

The first two introductory sections recount how "the law" was given to mankind in the context of the creation of Ahura Mazda and the counter-creation of Angra Mainyu, and how Yima, the founder of civilization, refused to transmit "the law" to human beings. The next sixteen sections deal chiefly with religious, civil, criminal, and purification laws. The three sections appended at the end are of a mythical character dealing with the feats of Zoroaster and the origin of three types of medicine: one that heals with the knife, one with herbs, and one with sacred spells. The following is a summary of the twenty-two sections.

Fargard 1 introduces and describes the sixteen creations of the different regions of Iran by Ahura Mazda, and the sixteen counter creations of plagues by Angra Mainyu (the Adversary).

Fargard 2 has two parts. The first is in honour of Yima, king of the Golden Age, who refused to accept and transmit "the law" to humanity; instead, he made human beings prosperous and immortal. The second is a narration of Yima, who, at the request of Ahura

Mazda, built a fortified enclosure to preserve all living creatures from an approaching severe winter.

Fargard 3–12 deals essentially with legal aspects: laws related to the proper cultivation of the earth, the practice of medicine, signing contracts, contact with corpses, and procedures for purification.

Fargard 13–14 consists of a praise to the dog and the crime of killing one, especially a water dog.

Fargard 15–17 deals with laws related to pregnancy, adultery, abortion, "mortal" sins, and breeding dogs.

Fargard 18 deals with miscellaneous laws, the breaking of which makes the Lie (*Druj*) prosper with his demons; with the evil that derives from a prostitute (*jahi*); and with the treatment of uncleanliness due to sexual intercourse with a menstruating woman.

Fargard 19 recounts the feats of Zoroaster: how he defended himself against the attacks of the demons with stones, sacred words, and sacrificial implements given him by Ahura Mazda; how he was instructed by Ahura Mazda on "the good religion," including its rites and prescriptions; how the mysteries of the spiritual world were revealed to him; and how he finally routed the demons by invoking the creation of Ahura Mazda.

Fargard 20–22 deals with three means of effective healing: herbs, sacred spells, and the knife.

The following selections from the Videvdat give a general idea of the development of Zoroastrian laws, which must have taken the labours of several generations of thinkers.[8]

Videvdat III.3

14 (44). Let no man alone by himself carry a corpse. If a man alone by himself carry a corpse, the Nasu [corpse-demon] rushes upon him, to defile him, from the nose of the dead, from the eye, from the tongue, from the jaws, from the sexual organ, from the hinder parts. This Drug, this Nasu, falls upon him, stains him even to the end of the nails, and he is unclean, thenceforth, for ever and ever.

Videvdat III.4

38 (130). O Maker of the material world, thou Holy One! If a man shall bury in the earth either the corpse of a dog or the corpse of a man, and if he shall not disinter it within the second year, what is the penalty for it? What is the atonement for it? What is the cleansing from it?

39 (135). Ahura Mazda answered: "For that deed there is nothing that can pay, nothing that can atone, nothing that can cleanse from it; it is a trespass for which there is no atonement, for ever and ever."

Videvdat V.6

27 (82). O Maker of the material world, thou Holy One! If there be a number of men resting in the same place ... and of those people one happens to die; how many of them does the Drug Nasu envelope with infection, pollution, and uncleanness?

28 (86). Ahura Mazda answered: "If the dead one be a priest, the Drug Nasu rushes forth, O Spitama Zarathustra! she falls on the eleventh and defiles the ten. If the dead one be a warrior, the Drug Nasu rushes forth, O Spitama Zarathustra! she falls on the tenth and defiles the nine. If the dead one be a husbandman ... she falls on the ninth and defiles the eight. If it be a shepherd's dog ... she falls on the eighth and defiles the seven. If it be a house dog ... she falls on the seventh and defiles the six ..."

Videvdat VII.10

73 (183). O Maker of the material world, thou Holy One! Can the eating vessels be made clean that have been touched by the carcass of a dog, or by the corpse of a man?

74 (184). Ahura Mazda answered: "They can, O holy Zarathustra!"
How so?

"If they be of gold, you shall wash them once with gomez [consecrated urine of the ox], you shall rub them once with earth, you shall wash them once with water, and they shall be clean. If they be of silver, you shall wash them twice with gomez, you shall rub them twice with earth, you shall wash them twice with water, and they shall be clean. If they be of brass, you shall wash them thrice with gomez, you shall rub them thrice with earth, you shall wash them thrice with water, and they shall be clean. If they be of steel, you shall wash them four times ... If they be of stone, you shall wash them six times ... If they be of earth, of wood, or of clay, they are unclean for ever and ever."

Videvdat VIII.2

8 (21). "Whosoever shall smite either a shepherd's dog, or a house dog, or a Vohunazga dog [dog without a master], or a hunting dog, his soul when passing to the other world, shall fly amid louder howling and fiercer pursuing than the sheep does when the wolf rushes upon it in the lofty forest."

9 (24) "No soul will come and meet his departing soul and help it through the howls and pursuit in the other world; nor will the dogs that keep the Kinvad [Chinvat] bridge help his departing soul through the howls and pursuit in the other world."

Videvdat XVI.3

17 (39). "Whosoever shall lie in sexual intercourse with a woman who has an issue of blood, either out of the ordinary course or at the usual period,

does no better deed than if he should burn the corpse of his own son, born of his own body and dead of naeza [possibly spear or disease], and drop its fat into the fire."

18 (41). "All such sinners, embodiments of the Drug, are scorners of the law; all scorners of the law are rebels against the Lord; all rebels against the Lord are ungodly men; and any ungodly man shall pay for it with his life."

Khordeh Avesta

The Khordeh Avesta (Little Avesta) is often combined with the Yasht in the form of a single text and is intended for the use of priests and lay persons in private devotion, or during public services. Its contents are taken from other parts of the Avesta, mainly from the Yasna and Yasht, and consist of the following principal sections:

Nyaishe: five short prayers addressed to the sun, moon, water, fire, and angels who preside over these elements.

Gah: five prayers devoted to the spirits or genii presiding over the five divisions of each day.

Siroze (*Sirozah*): invocations enumerating the thirty divinities, or spiritual beings, each of whom is believed to preside over one day of the month, and by whose names the days are called.

Afringan: words of blessings, numerous in number, used at certain fixed times during the year. The following list represents the four different forms of Afringan and their respective occasions of use.

- *Afringan Dahman,* in honour of the dead.
- *Afringan Gatha,* in honour of the five concluding days of the year, when the souls of the dead revisit the earth.
- *Afringan Gahambar,* in honour of the celebration of the six seasonal feasts of the year (each feast lasts for five days), commemorating the different acts of creation.
- *Afringan Rapithwin,* in honour of the beginning and end of summer, and in honour of the spirit presiding over the southern quarter of the hemisphere, who is the guardian spirit of the path to paradise.

The following few selections will indicate the nature of the Khordeh Avesta:[9]

Gah I

1. I confess myself a Mazda-worshipper, of Zarathustra's order, a foe to the Daevas [Demons], devoted to the lore of the Lord, for the holy Havani

[first division of the day, 6–10 a.m.], regulator of the ritual order, for its sacrifice, homage, propitiation, and praise ...

Gah V

1. I confess myself a Mazda-worshipper, of the order of Zarathustra, a foe to the Daevas, devoted to the lore of the Lord, for the Ushahina [fifth division of the day: 12 p.m. – 6 a.m.], sacrifice, homage, propitiation, and praise ...

Afringan Gahambar

19. And I bless in my prayer the sacrifice, and homage, and the strength, and swiftness of the day-lords during daylight, and of the lords of the days in their length, of the month-lords, and the year-lords, and of the lords of the seasons (in their course), and for the worship, homage, propitiation, and praise of the lofty lord who is the Righteous Ritual itself, and of those lords of the ritual who are of all the greatest ...

Yasht

The Yasht (meaning "act of devotion" or "worship") is a collection of twenty-one invocations or hymns, plus a few fragmentary sections appended at the end. The main parts of the Yasht consist of prayers addressed to angels and various deities of differing ranks (for whom days of the month are named), and to genii who preside over the five divisions of each day. The basic difference between the prayers in the Yasht and those in the Yasna or Visparad is that each of the prayers in the Yasht is devoted to the praise and worship of one divine being only, or of a certain limited class of divine beings, whereas those in the Yasna or Visparad invoke indiscriminately. In addition, the Yasht contains blessings for various occasions, notably for honouring the souls of the departed.

The following summary will give an idea of the contents of the Yasht.

Yasht 1 is addressed to Ahura Mazda, enumerating his twenty names, the recitation of which is considered to be efficacious against all dangers.

Yasht 2 is addressed to the seven Amesha Spenta (Holy Immortals) and is usually recited on each of the seven days of the week consecrated to them.

Yasht 3 is devoted to the praise of Asha-Vahishta (Best Righteousness), which is described as driving away all the evil spells (plagues and diseases) brought upon the world by Angra Mainyu (Evil Spirit).

Yasht 4 refers to Haurvatat (Health or Wholeness) and to the proper performance of the Bareshnum ceremony, as being the test of the true Zoroastrian.

Yasht 5 is devoted to Ardvi Sura Anahita, the great goddess of the heavenly spring from which all waters on earth flow down from the top of Hukairya, the mythical mountain in the region of the stars.

Yasht 6–21 is devoted respectively to the following male and female divine powers: Sun, Moon, Stars, Cow (personification of the animal kingdom), Mithra, Sraosha, Rashnu, the Fravashi, Verethraghna, Vayu, Kishta (or Cista, Din, Daena), Ashi Vanguhi, Arshtat, Zamyad, Haoma, and Vanant.

The fragmentary sections appended at the end describe the fate of the soul after death, the words of blessings pronounced by Zoroaster to King Vishtaspa, and the account of how Zoroaster gave King Vishtaspa a summary of "the law."

Some of these Yashts are recited every day (such as Yasht 1); others are recited on special occasions, or on particular days (such as Yasht 2). The following selections from the Yasht will give an idea of the devotional recitations or sacred acts of worship.[10]

Yasht 1

1. Zarathustra asked Ahura Mazda: O Ahura Mazda, most beneficent Spirit, Creator of the material world, righteous! What (aspect) of Holy Word is most powerful? What is most defensive (?) (victorious)? What is most glorious? What is bravest?

3. Then Ahura Mazda said: Our name [i.e, Amesha Spentas], O Spitamid Zarathushtra, is what is most powerful of the Holy Word, that (name is) most victorious, that (name is) most glorious, most brave …

5. Then Zarathustra said: Declare to me, O righteous Ahura Mazda, that name of yours which is the greatest and the most beautiful and the most victorious and the most curative and the best at overcoming the hostility of daewas and (evil) men …

7. Then Ahura Mazda said: (First) I am called "He Who Is to Be Implored," O righteous Zarathustra; second, "Shepherd" (?); third, … (?); fourth, "Asha Washishta"; fifth, "All the Good Created by Mazda, the Seed of Asha"; sixth, I am "Intelligence"; seventh, "Intelligent"; eighth, I am "Insight"; ninth, "Insightful";

8. tenth, I am "Beneficence"; eleventh, "Possessing Beneficence"; twelfth, "Lord" (Ahura); thirteenth, "Invincible"; sixteenth, "He Who Remembers

(People's) Merit"; seventeenth, "All Perceiving"; eighteenth, "Curative";
nineteenth, I am "Creator"; twentieth, I am called "Mazda."

10. If, O Zarathushtra, you want to overcome those hostilities (of) daewas
and men, (of) sorcerers and witches, (of) tyrants, kawis, and karapans, (of)
biped scoundrels and biped distorters of Truth and quadruped wolves,

11. and the hostile army with a broad front, with a broad banner, then recite these names during all the days and nights.

Yasht 5

1. Ahura Mazda said to Zarathushtra Spitama: On my account, worship
her, O Zarathushtra Spitama, Aredwi Sura Anahita who spreads abroad, is
healing, opposed to daewas, a follower of ahuric doctrine, who is worthy to
be worshipped by the material world (and) worthy to be praised by the material world, who is a crop-increasing ashawan, a herd-increasing ashawan,
and ashawan who makes the country prosper,

2. who purifies the semen of all males, who purifies for conception the
wombs of all females, who gives easy delivery to all females, who gives milk
to all females regularly and at the proper time;

3. (worship her), the vast, famed afar, who is as great as all these waters
which flow forth upon the earth, who forcefully flows forth from Mount
Hukairya ...

Yasht 10

1. Ahura Mazda said to Zarathushtra the Spitamid: When I created
Mithra of wide pastures, I made him, O Spitamid, as worthy of worship and
praise as myself, Ahura Mazda.

6. With libations I shall worship the powerful god, strong Mithra, strongest in the (world of) creatures; I shall pay homage to him with praise and
reverence; with libations I shall audibly worship him, Mithra of wide pastures ...

Yasht 17

1. We worship good Ashi (who is) regal, tall, beautiful, good to be worshipped...

2. the daughter of Ahura Mazda, the sister of Amesha Spentas ....

6. O good Ashi, O beautiful Ashi, O radiant Ashi, shining joyfully with
(your) rays! O Ashi, (you who) give good fortune to these men whom you
accompany!

VERSIONS

The difficulty in understanding the two dialects used in the composition of the Avesta (Gathic and Avestan) at the time of the Sasanids

necessitated a translation of the text into Pahlavi (Middle Persian), an alphabet that was widely known.[11] The Pahlavi version that is now extant (more commonly known as Zend or Zand) includes the entire Yasna, Visparad, Videvdat, and some parts from the remaining sections of the Avesta.

The Pahlavi rendering is a word-for-word translation of the Avesta, with the occasional addition of short explanatory notes, plus the occasional long, digressive commentary on the text. These additional exegetical portions, including the works of interpretation, derive probably from a period after the Islamic conquest of Iran. They are "largely expressive of religious ideas and institutions tenaciously held in the course of some two centuries [ca. 9th-10th] of declining fortunes."[12] Their greatest value lies in their help in determining the meaning of a word or phrase or some obscure idea in the Avesta, even though some of the additional explanations are fanciful. Their chief defect lies in their clumsy handling of the principles of grammar, resulting in numerous inaccuracies and errors.

Sometime during the 1200s, a large segment of the Pahlavi version was translated into Sanskrit by a Zoroastrian priest called Neryosangh, son of Dhaval. His knowledge of the Pahlavi language seems to be thorough, and his translation is of great help in understanding obscure passages in the Pahlavi version. In addition to the Sanskrit version, there are three translations of portions of the Pahlavi version: a modern Persian translation, whose date may be assigned to the period between 1600 and 1800 of this era, and two separate translations into Gujarati, both of which date from 1818. These modern versions are occasionally consulted to clarify some obscure or ambiguous word or passage in the Pahlavi version.

OTHER RELIGIOUS DOCUMENTS

There are a great many other documents written in Pahlavi for which no Avesta equivalent is known. These Pahlavi writings date from the third to the eleventh century CE. Their contents are entirely of a religious and theological character (including those that contain historical legends) and basically embody the Zoroastrian beliefs during the Sasanid age. At least fifty-five works are known, of which the following are the most important.

Bundahishn

The book usually known as the Bundahishn (meaning Primal Creation) survives in two versions: a long version known as the Greater or Iranian Bundahishn, and a short version known as the Indian Bundahishn.[13] The complete work consists of thirty-six chapters.

The Bundahishn begins with a cosmogony. In the beginning is both Ahura Mazda, the omniscient, good spirit existing in the state of endless light, and Ahriman, the witless, evil spirit existing in the state of endless darkness. Both produce their own kind of creatures. The first beings created by Ahura Mazda are the six Amesha Spenta. Corresponding with each of them is a demon created by Ahriman. Then Ahura Mazda creates the sky, water, earth, plants, the ox (representing the animal kingdom), Gayomard (the Zoroastrian Adam, representing humanity), and the constellations. Each of Ahura Mazda's creations is opposed and destroyed by Ahriman.

Then follows a series of discussions describing the following: the terrestrial world – countries, mountains, seas, rivers, lakes, trees, birds, wind, cloud, rain, animals, humanity, sleep, and sound; the year, seasons, days, and their parts; the role of each divine power worshipped during the year, and the role of Ahriman and his demons; the fate of the soul after death; the six millennia and their respective calamities preceding the end of the world; prophecies dealing with the resurrection of the body; and the twelve millennia associated with the twelve signs of the Zodiac.

The concluding chapters give the genealogies of Persian kings and heroes, of Zoroaster and certain priests, together with an account of Persian chronology from the moment of creation to the period of the Arab conquest.

The following few selections will indicate the nature of the book.[14]

Bundahishn 1

1. Thus is it revealed in the Good Religion. Ohrmazd [Ahura Mazda] was on high in omniscience and goodness; for infinite time he was ever in the light. The light is the space and place of Ohrmazd: some call it the Endless Light ...

2. Ahriman, slow in knowledge, whose will is to smite, was deep down in darkness; (he was) and is, yet will not be. The will to smite is his permanent disposition, and darkness is his place: some call it the Endless Darkness.

5. Ohrmazd, in his omniscience, knew that the Destructive Spirit existed, that he would attack and, since his will is envy, would mingle with him ...

11. Then Ohrmazd, in his omniscience, knew that if he did not fix a time for battle against him, then Ahriman would do unto his creation even as he had threatened; and the struggle and the mixture would be everlasting ...

14. Then Ohrmazd chanted the *Ahunvar*, that is he recited the twenty-one words of the *Yatha ahu vairyo*: and he showed to the Destructive Spirit his own final victory, the powerlessness of the Destructive Spirit, the destruc-

tion of the demons, the resurrection, the Final Body, and the freedom of creation from all aggression for ever and ever.

15. When the Destructive Spirit beheld his own powerlessness and the destruction of the demons, he was laid low, swooned, and fell back into the darkness ...

16. While Ahriman lay crushed Ohrmazd created his creation. First he fashioned forth Vahuman (the Good Mind) ... The Destructive Spirit first created the Lying Word and then Akoman (the Evil Mind) ...

18. Of the material creation Ohrmazd (fashioned forth) first the sky, second water, third earth, fourth plants, fifth cattle, and sixth Man.

Bundahishn 14

1. (Ohrmazd) says in the Religion: "I created man in ten species. First was he who is bright and white-eyed, even Gayomart. Of the ten species one is Gayomart, and the (other) nine proceeded from him. The tenth is the monkey, the lowest of men."

2. When Gayomart passed away and let fall his seed, that seed was purified by the light of the Sun: two parts of it were preserved by Neryosang [a messenger deity] and one part was received by Spandarmat (the Earth). For forty years it remained in the earth. When the forty years had elapsed, Mashye and Mashyane grew out of the earth in the form of a rhubarb plant ...

4. Then the two of them (Mashye and Mashyane) developed from plant form into human form, and the *khwarr* which is their soul entered into them secretly ...

5. Ohrmazd said to Mashye and Mashyane: "Ye are men, the father (and mother) of the world; do ye your works in accordance with righteous order and a perfect mind. Think, speak, and do what is good. Do not worship the Demons."

Shayest ne-Shayest

The writings known as Shayest ne-Shayest (also known as Pahlavi Rivayats) are of a character different from the Bundahishn. The term "shayest" and its antonym "ne-shayest" mean "proper" or "fit" and "improper" or "unfit," respectively. The text is a compilation of miscellaneous laws and customs regarding sin and impurity, with details of rules about ritual and ceremonies and those who can and cannot perform them. The subjects are so varied that only a few examples will be selected for illustration.[15]

Shayest ne-Shayest 2

8. Every one who understands the care of a corpse is proper; two boys of eight years old, who understand the care, are proper; a woman free from

menstruation, or free from dead matter, or a man, with a woman or a child of eight years old, is proper.

63. Whoever brings dead matter to any person is worthy of death; he is thrice worthy of death at the time when a dog has not seen the corpse; and if through negligence of appliances and means he disturbs it, and disturbs it by touching it, he knows that it is a sin worthy of death ...

65. When they move a corpse which a dog has not seen with a thousand men, even then the bodies of the whole number are polluted, and are to be washed for them with ceremony.

76. Any one who, through sinfulness, throws a corpse into the water, is worthy of death on the spot ...

77. Of the water, into which one throws dead matter, the extent of pollution is three steps of three feet in the water advancing, nine steps of three feet in the water passed over, and six steps of three feet in the depth of the water, and three steps of three feet in the water pouring over the dead matter are polluted as regards the depth.

Shayest ne-Shayest 4

1. A sacred thread-girdle, should it be made of silk, is not proper; the hair of a hairy goat and a hairy camel is proper, and from other hairy creatures it is proper among the lowly ...

11. A girdle to which there is no fringe is proper; and when they shall tie a woman's ringlet [hair loose down to her waist] it is not proper.

Shayest ne-Shayest 6

1. The deaf and dumb and helpless, though of unblemished conduct and proper disposition, is incapable of doing good works, and from the time when he is born till the time when he shall die, all the good works which they may perform in the world become his property as much as his even by whom they are performed.

Shayest ne-Shayest 8

1. Sin which affects accusers is to be atoned for among the accusers, and that relating to the soul is to be atoned for among the high-priests, and when they do whatever the high-priests of the religion command the sin will depart, and the good works which they may thenceforth do will attain completion. The sin of him who is worthy of death is to be confessed unto the high-priests, and he is to deliver up his body; except to the high-priests he is not to deliver up his body.

Shayest ne-Shayest 10

19. The rule is this, that a man, when he does not wed a wife, does not become worthy of death; but when a woman does not wed a husband it

amounts to a sin worthy of death; because for a woman there is no offspring except by intercourse with men, and no lineage proceeds from her; but for a man without a wife, when he shall recite the Avesta, as it is mentioned in the Vendidad [Videvdat], there may be a lineage which proceeds onwards to the future existence.

Shayest ne-Shayest 20

8. This, too, that the walks of men are to be directed chiefly to these three places; to the abode of the well-informed, to the abode of the good, and to the abode of the fires [i.e., fire-temple].

Shkand Gumanig Wizar

The Shkand Gumanig Wizar (literally meaning "doubt-dispelling explanations") is a defensive presentation or apology for the Zoroastrian religion vis-à-vis Islam, Judaism, Christianity, and Manichaeism. The author of this book is a certain Mardan-Farrukh (Martanfarrux) who lived in Persia long after the Arab conquest. He states (in chapter 10.43–63) that he is a Zoroastrian not so much by birth as by conviction. It seemed to him that the Zoroastrian faith offered the only reasonable explanation for all the perennial enigmas, including the origin and existence of evil. He therefore marshals his arguments in favour of Zoroastrian dualism by attacking the inconsistencies inherent in the teachings of other faiths. The following selections are self-explanatory and illustrate the author's objective. [16]

Shkand Gumanig Wizar 10

38. And I observed, in the world, the sectarian belief of all maintainers of sects who hold the two fundamental doctrines.

39. One is that which asserts that all the good and evil, which are in the world, are owing to the sacred being [god].

40. The other is that which asserts that all the good of the world, besides the hope of preserving the soul, is owing to the sacred being; (41) and the cause of all evil of the body, besides the risk of the soul, is owing to Aharman ...

43. Now I have been an enquirer everywhere, for understanding the sacred being ... (44) as likewise I have wandered, for the sake of investigation, to the region without and the land of the Hindus, and to many different races ...

46. I sought that which was more steadfast and more acceptable in wisdom and testimony.

61. I have been deliberately confirmed by the power of wisdom and the strength of knowledge of the religion, (62) not through obstinate faith, but

by the pure revelation opposed to the demon [i.e., the Videvdat = the anti-demonic law] which is the decision of Auharmazd, (63) that was taught by the creator Auharmazd to the righteous Zartust [Zoroaster].

Shkand Gumanig Wizar 11

1. Henceforth I write of the inconsistency of their twaddle, and of just observations (2) you should estimate with wise regard.

3. First, as to the full consideration of that one original evolution (4) which they [i.e., Muslims] state thus: "The sacred being is one, doing good works, wise, powerful, compassionate, and merciful, (5) so that good works and crime, truth and falsehood, life and death, good and evil are owing to him" [cf. Qur'an 64.13, 64.18; 30.39].

6. Now do ye ask of them (7) thus: "Is the sacred being always compassionate and showing mercy, doing good works and judicious, and does he know all that is, was, and will be ... ?

8. "Because, if he be compassionate, doing good works, and showing mercy, why then are Aharman and the demons and all these evil faiths of hell admitted by him to his own creatures, through his own compassion, doing of good works, and showing of mercy?"

9. "If not known by him, where are that knowledge and omniscience of his?"

Shkand Gumanig Wizar 13

1. Again, about the inconsistency and faulty statements of the first scripture [i.e., the Old Testament], (2) which they call holy – (3) and as to it they are, in every way, unanimous that the sacred being wrote it with his own hand, and gave it to Moses – (4) so that, as it is full of delusion, I will here publish, for your information, a story out of all its stupidity and of much that is in it.

5. It states, in the beginning of the scripture, (6) that there first arose earth, without form and void, darkness and black water; (7) and the breathing of the sacred being ever yearns over the face of that black water [cf. Genesis 1:1–2].

12. In six days this world and sky and earth were also created by him, (13) for during the seventh day he was reposing and comfortable [cf. Genesis 1:4–5, 31; 2:1–2].

14. Through that same mystery even now the Jews are enjoying repose on the Sabbath day [cf. Exodus 20:10–11].

92. Again, I ask this ... (94) when this world was not produced by him from anything, but merely arose by his command, "thou shalt arise," and it was so, (95) to what was that delay of his of six days owing?

96. For when his trouble is merely as much as to say, "thou shalt arise," the existence of that delay of six days is very ill-seeming.

102. I also ask this, to what was it owing that it was necessary for him to make himself comfortable and reposing on the seventh day?

Shkand Gumanig Wizar 15

1. Another thing I publish is a feeble story about the inconsistency, unbounded statements, and incoherent disputations of Christian believers.

2. Since, inasmuch as all three are from the one origin of Judaism – (4) you should know whence the original sect of Christianity came forth.

5. That in the town of Jerusalem there was a woman of the same Jews who was known for misconduct, (6) and pregnancy became manifest in her.

7. When asked by them thus: "Whence is this pregnancy of thine?" (8) she said in reply thus: "The angel Gabriel came unto me, and he spoke thus: 'Thou art pregnant by the pure wind (holy spirit)'" [cf. Matthew 1:18; Luke 1:26–27, 35].

9. As to that, you should observe thus: "Who apart from that woman, saw the angel Gabriel? And on what account is it expedient to consider that woman truthful?"

18. Observe, again, that if they say the Messiah arose from the pure wind of the sacred being [i.e., Holy Spirit of God], that implies … that the other wind, which is distinct from that, is not from the sacred being and not pure, (19) and another producer is manifested inevitably.

31. And there are some even who say that the Messiah is the sacred being himself.

32. Now this is very strange, when the mighty sacred being, the maintainer and cherisher of the two existences, became of human nature, and went into the womb of a woman who was a Jew.

33. To leave the lordly throne, the sky and earth, the celestial sphere and other similar objects of his management and protection, he fell for concealment, into a polluted and straitened place, (34) and, finally, delivered his own body to scourging, execution on the tree at the hands of the enemies, (35) while, apart from death, much brutality and lawlessness were arranged by them.

46. Again, as to this which they state, that the father and son and pure wind are three names which are not separate one from the other, (47) nor is one foremost, (48) and this, too, that, though a son, he is not less than the father, but in every knowledge equal to the father [cf. Athanasian Creed], why now is one to call him by a different name? (49) If it be proper for three to be one, that implies that it is certainly possible for three to be nine and for nine to be three; (50) and it is possible to speak of other number, in this sequence, unlimitedly.

Shkand Gumanig Wizar 16

1. Again, about the delusion of Mani, one out of the thousands and myr-

iads is written; (2) for I am not unrestrained as to writing more fully of the delusion, twaddle, and deceit of Mani and the Manichaeans ...

4. Now you Mazda-worshippers of Zaratust should know that the original statement of Mani was about the unlimitedness of the original evolutions, (5) the intermediate one about their mingling, (6) and the final one about the distinction of light from dark, (7) that which is much more like unto want of distinction.

53. Now I speak first about the impossibility of the occurrence of any existing thing that is unlimited, (54) except only those which I call unlimited, that is, empty space and time.

55. Those, indeed, which are for existence within them – that is beings and things in locality and time – are seen to be limited.

Denkard

The Denkard (Denkart, Dinkard, meaning "Acts of Religion") is an encyclopaedic account of history, literature, religious doctrines, legend, customs, and traditions, compiled and written in the ninth century CE by a Zoroastrian high priest called Adurbad-i Emetan. The extant Denkard consists of seven books (Books 3–9); the first two books are lost, as is the beginning of Book 3.

Books 3–5 are generally grouped together because their focus of discussion is primarily to defend the Zoroastrian faith by refuting on rational grounds other religious traditions. Thus, these three books contain an exposition of Zoroastrian beliefs, doctrines, and practices; a description of the division and development of human races; a history of scriptures; an account of the life of Zoroaster; and an explication of the misdeeds of Ahriman and his agents.

Book 6 contains moral instructions, rules of conduct, characteristics of good and evil, and religious maxims.

Book 7 gives an account of the life of Zoroaster and of the events following his time; of the coming of saviours to fight against evil; of the appearance of a final saviour, who will bring about the ultimate defeat of evil and restore the world to its pristine purity and peace.

Book 8 contains a summary of the lost twenty-one nasks originally contained in the Avesta.

Book 9 paraphrases parts of Avesta writings on religious doctrine and practice.

The following extracts from Book 6 constitute the most important exposition of the Zoroastrian faith during the late Sasanid and early Muslim Arab period.[17]

Denkard 6

138. They held this too: One ought to pay much heed to these several things: a man of good fame, a day of good fame and a work of good fame.

163. They held this too: The mind of religion is Zoroaster, the mind of righteousness is the sacred word, the mind of Iranian dignity is the position of the ruler.

216. They held this too: there is no one who is a greater enemy to religion than heretics ... The heretic enters across the outermost wall in guise of one who carries the sacred word: Some come even up to the selfless and nearness of the religion.

A6b Consider this too, O men: from every thing there is a way of escape, except from death; every thing can be controlled, except wickedness; every thing is transient, except righteousness; every thing can be disciplined, except substance; every thing can be turned away, except the decree of the gods.

B1 It is manifest: Every good thing was created by Ohrmazd and every bad thing was created by Ahreman.

B7 This too is manifest: The best thing is truthfulness, the worst thing is lie.

C67 This too is thus: From righteous effort there comes about righteous action, and from righteous action it is easier for a man to maintain his property so that it should last longer.

C68 This too is thus: From sinful effort there comes about sinful action, and because of sinful action a man destroys his property.

D1b A man who performs the worship of the gods with certainty as to the gods and with (faith in) the reality of the thing, is a son of the gods and his place is in the highest heaven ... A man who performs the worship of the gods with the thought that the gods do not exist and that the thing does not exist, is an enemy of the gods and his place is in Hell.

D9 They say concerning the same Adurbad that he said: Every person ought to know: "Where have I come from? For what purpose am I here? Where do I return?" I, for my part, know that I come from Ohrmazd the Lord, that I am here so as to make the demons powerless, and that I shall return to Ohrmazd.

SCRIPTURE AND TRADITION

The Avesta or the Zend (translation of the Avesta in Pahlavi with commentary) serve at the present day as the authoritative, holy scriptures of the Zoroastrians. To them, they contain the teachings of Zoroaster and the answer to almost all practical needs of life. To be sure, even in its present fragmentary form, the Avesta is one of the great religious monuments of antiquity. It preserves the records of a faith that might well have been a legacy to the West. But the defeat of the Persians at the hands of first the Macedonians and then the Arabs dealt a crippling blow to the Zoroastrians and their scriptures. Indeed, it is a wonder that the Avesta was not destroyed altogether. Today, the texts that have been preserved in the Avesta represent the fundamental tenets of the Zoroastrian faith.

The authority of the remaining group of religious writings in Pahlavi, however, is open to dispute. These writings contain the opinions and decisions of Zoroastrian high priests of later times. Nonetheless, they have an inestimable value for supplying numerous details of religious customs and traditions that cannot be found elsewhere, and for giving an insight into the Zoroastrian beliefs and practices of the times preceding and following the Muslim Arab invasion. Thus, both scripture and tradition have positive values, and a judicious balance of these two will undoubtedly produce more rewarding results for those seeking to understand the Zoroastrian faith.

CHAPTER FOUR

Zoroastrian Teachings

The task of making sense of the content and ideas set out in the Avesta and in the other Zoroastrian scriptural documents is at once both easy and difficult. Easy, because the subject matter is reasonably manageable, and various Zoroastrian beliefs and practices have remained substantially unchanged. Difficult, because contemporary exponents of the Zoroastrian tradition are divided, with respect to their position, understanding, and interpretation of the Avesta and other religious documents, into two groups: the orthodox, who defend tradition; and the reformist, who insist on change. Lack of agreement, however, has had little effect on the fundamental issues of faith; controversy has centred primarily on the form of religious practices. As yet, no drastic changes have been accepted in response to the challenges posed by reformists.

The following, then, is an analysis of some of the more important Zoroastrian ideas, based primarily on the documents mentioned above.

AHURA MAZDA

The name of the supreme God of the Zoroastrian faith is Ahura Mazda (or Ohrmazd). He is self-created, omniscient, omnipresent, holy, invisible, and beyond human conceptualization (Yasna 4.7, 29.4, 31.13, 45.5; Yasht 1.7, 1.8, 1.12, 1.13–14; Videvdat 2.1, 19.20). He is neither begotten, nor is there anyone who is his equal. He is, as his name implies, the Wise Lord, the Most Knowing One, and the Most Far-Seeing One (Yasna 29.6, 33.13, 45.3, 46.19, 48.2–3). In fact, in a passage recorded in the Avesta, Ahura Mazda says of himself: "My sixth name is Understanding; my seventh is Intelligent One; my eighth name is Knowledge; my ninth is Endowed With Knowledge;

my twentieth is Mazda (Wisdom). I am the Wise One; my name is the Wisest of the Wise" (Yasht 1.7, 1.8, 1.15).

This infinite wisdom, or omniscience, is absolute, so that he knows everything before it happens (Yasna 43.6, 45.4). Consequently, he is all-pervading, and there is no conceivable place where he is not. He is also changeless, first and foremost, the most perfect being, the greatest, the most powerful, the one who was, is, and will be forever (Yasna 1.1, 28.8, 31.7, 43.4, 45.10).

Ahura Mazda is the creator of the universe, the author of the celestial and terrestrial worlds (Yasna 31.7, 50.11). He has brought forth rivers, trees, forests, wind, clouds, sun, moon, stars, and the seasons (Yasna 44.3–5; 51–7). He guards heaven and earth from falling, and everything follows the sequence he has ordained from the beginning. He created the human body and endowed it with life, mind, and conscience (Yasna 31.11). He is the dispenser of every material good and spiritual blessing, because it is in his nature to be beneficent to all his creation.

As the sovereign lord of all existence and as the creator and sustainer of the entire universe, he rules according to his own will (Yasna 28.7, 29.6, 45.3, 48.2–3). He is a friend and helper of human beings, deeply interested in their welfare (Yasna 28.11, 31.21, 43.1–3, 46.2). Hence, the righteous praise him with one accord as their father and lord, while the entire creation sings to his glory. Even the wicked who have been led astray by Ahriman (the Adversary) will ultimately seek his grace and mercy.

Anthropomorphic traits are more rarely attributed to Ahura Mazda in the Avesta than they are to the God of the Bible. When they are suggested, however, they are not to be taken literally but regarded as symbolic expressions or poetic licence. Thus, he is spoken of as living in the heavenly realm and dwelling in the straight paths of righteousness, wearing the firmament as his garment (Yasna 28.5, 30.5, 33.5). Again, he is conceived of as observing with his eyes everything that is done in secret or in the open, and as distributing to human beings their just dues by his own hands (Yasna 31.13, 43.4). And again, he is spoken of as the one who proclaims the truth directly through the mouth of his prophet, indeed through the prophet's tongue, in order that the prophet may be able to convince human beings of Ahura Mazda's truth.

Hence, Zoroastrian tradition maintains that Ahura Mazda revealed to Zoroaster the secrets or mysteries of creation; the realities of life after death; the unseen, spiritual powers that dwell in, around, and above the world; and the requirements of what constitutes a good life. Devout followers of Ahura Mazda contemplate and enumerate the following divine or honorific titles: maker, radiant, glorious, the greatest, the best, the most beautiful, the most firm, the most wise, of the most perfect form, the highest in righteousness, possessed of great joy, creator, fashioner, sustainer, and the most Holy Spirit (Yasna 1.1). Ahura Mazda is synonymous with light, and the sun is spoken of as his most beautiful form (Yasna 36.6, 58.8); in fact, it is called his eye (Yasna 1.11). "Radiant" and "glorious" are the two epithets most frequently used in the Avesta as an opening invocation to the divinity. The first Yasht, which is dedicated to him, enumerates seventy-four of these attributes, all descriptive of his wisdom, power, justice, righteousness, and mercy.

Through his wisdom Ahura Mazda guides the faithful in the path of righteousness (Denkard, SAN vol. 3, p. 174). He alone knows the inmost recesses of the human heart and therefore is the best judge of human thoughts, words, and deeds (Bundahishn 1.13, 17, 20; Zadspram 1.2; Denkard, SAN vol. 7, p. 473). Despite his rival, Ahriman, who always disrupts his work, Ahura Mazda is not wanting in anything, and is to be regarded as the invisible, omnipotent, supreme being to whom the faithful can turn for protection and help (Shkand Gumanig Wizar 1.1; Denkard, SAN vol. 1, p. 34; vol. 2, p. 103; vol. 3, p. 140, 157; vol. 7, p. 440). Through his wisdom he exercises his providential care to maintain the world he created. Since he is father and lord of creation, all good creatures, including human beings, perform their sacred duty by obeying his divine command (Denkard, SAN vol. 4, p. 268; vol. 5, pp. 323–4).

Ahura Mazda is the eternal source of all blessings and benefactions. To those who turn to him in joy and sorrow, and who trust in his infinite goodness, he is all merciful. His goodness extends to the good and evil alike, for his nature can never contemplate evil of any kind (Menog i Xrad 8.22, 38.4; Zadspram 1.17; Dadastan i Dinig 37.127). He knows the infirmities of human nature caused by his adversary and therefore forgives the transgressions of the penitent. He is the divine law-giver and sovereign judge; naturally, his justice demands that each person receive his or her just dues. Rebels, therefore, have little hope of receiving reward from Ahura Mazda. Nevertheless, the wicked are not lost forever. For the all-merciful Ahura Mazda will ultimately, at the end of time, redeem them from their sinful past.

Thus, to know Ahura Mazda is to live in accordance with his divine will; to offer to him praise, worship, and devotion; to please him in purity of thought, word, and deed; to serve him not out of fear but out of love; and to further his cause by joining his forces to combat evil. Ahura Mazda has no beginning or end. His absolute nature, particularly his character of wisdom and goodness, remain unchanged forever.

SPENTA MAINYU

The relation between Ahura Mazda and Spenta Mainyu (Holy Spirit, Good Spirit, Bounteous Spirit) remains as subtle and elusive in the Avestan texts and Pahlavi versions as it is in the Gathas of Zoroaster. The name of Ahura Mazda is replaced in the Gathas by his appellative, Spenta Mainyu, who is in direct antagonism to Angra Mainyu (Evil Spirit). These two spirits are called twins in the Gathas and represent the good and evil aspects of existence respectively (Yasna 30.3–4, 45.2).

Several passages in the Avestan text speak of the "good creation" belonging to Spenta Mainyu (Yasna 57.17; Yasht 11.12, 13.76, 15.3, 15.43–44; Vendidad 3.20, 13.1, 13.2, 13.5, 13.6, 13.16). In fact, the stars are regarded as the creatures of Spenta Mainyu (Yasna 1.11, 12.32). And in a few instances Ahura Mazda is depicted as speaking of Spenta Mainyu as apart from himself (Yasht 13.12–13, 15.2–3). The Pahlavi versions also represent Spenta Mainyu as a being separate from, and created by, Ahura Mazda (Denkard, SAN vol. 2, p. 120; vol. 3, p. 158; vol. 4, pp. 194, 208, 209, 250–253; vol. 5, pp. 297, 326, 328, 340, 341, 348; vol. 8, pp. 441, 442, 474, 477).

However, an analysis of the appearances of the highly abstract concept of Spenta Mainyu in the Gathas, the Avesta, and the versions lead to the conclusion that Spenta Mainyu has no independent existence apart from Ahura Mazda. In other words, Spenta Mainyu is not to be conceived as a divine being but as a divine attribute of Ahura Mazda. As such, Spenta Mainyu is either jointly used with Ahura Mazda as God's distinguishing epithet, or presented alone by itself to designate or represent Ahura Mazda himself – just as the title His/Her Majesty represents a substitute for the name of a king or queen.

Furthermore, in the realm of "the Good," Spenta Mainyu alone is without his Fravashi (guardian spirit; see below for more discussion). Also, Spenta Mainyu does not receive homage and invocation from the faithful, as do Ahura Mazda and each of his ministering divine beings or angels. Consequently, Spenta Mainyu is to be regarded as a divine attribute of Ahura Mazda.

AMESHA SPENTA

As father and creator of all good things, Ahura Mazda created the two realms: the spiritual (*menog*), which cannot be seen, and the material (*getig*), which can be seen and is liable to destruction.[1] Of Ahura Mazda's mundane creations, the first was the sky, the second water, the third earth, the fourth vegetation, the fifth animals, the sixth mankind, and the seventh fire (Yasna 19.2, 19.4). Ahura Mazda's spiritual powers (sometimes thought of as archangels) consist of a group of six celestial beings called Amesha Spenta (or Amahraspand, meaning "Holy Immortal," or "Bountiful Immortal"), who stand second in rank to Ahura Mazda and together with Ahura Mazda at their head form a heptad – a number to which mystical potency is attributed (Yasna 27.15, 37.4, 35; Yasht 1.1–3, 2.13, 13.83, 19.16, 19.24–25).

The names of the six Amesha Spenta are: Vohu Manah, Asha Vahishta, Khshathra Vairya, Spenta Armaiti, Haurvatat, and Ameretat – the latter two being always closely united and generally mentioned together. The first three, Vohu Manah, Asha Vahishta, and Khshathra Vairya, are conceived of as masculine beings, though neuter in grammatical gender. Spenta Armaiti is represented as a feminine concept. Haurvatat and Ameretat are treated as masculine beings, though their grammatical gender is feminine. Their names are so sacred that one can use them to cast or break a spell (Yasht 1.3). In fact, to utter their name is synonymous with power and efficacy. An entire passage in the Avesta is devoted to their praise (Yasht 2).

Ahura Mazda created the Amesha Spenta to aid him in his work (Yasht 1.25, 2.1–3, 19.18). Each has a specific character and an assigned sphere to act on behalf, or as agent, of Ahura Mazda (Yasht 19.18–19, 28.7, 58.5). This means that each Amesha Spenta fulfils a twofold function: on the spiritual side each represents, or personifies, some specific virtue; and on the physical side each presides over some material object as its guardian spirit, or Fravashi. Accordingly, some material creation is consecrated to each Amesha Spenta.

A brief description, therefore, of the twofold function of each Amesha Spenta will help to understand the prominent place each holds in the Zoroastrian tradition.

Vohu Mana

Vohu Manah (or Vohuman, Bahman, meaning "Good Mind," "Best Mind") occupies and retains a pre-eminent position in the celestial hierarchy. As such, he is Ahura Mazda's first creation and the chief promoter of God's kingdom. He will eventually establish the divine kingdom at the command of Ahura Mazda (Yasna 30.8). Perfection (*haurvatat*) and immortality (*ameretat*) come from Ahura Mazda through Vohu Manah (Yasna 45.10). He embodies Ahura Mazda's good spirit and divine wisdom.[2]

Vohu Manah's wisdom (*khratu*) is usually classified into two distinct types: innate wisdom (*asna khratu*) and acquired wisdom (*gaoshosruta khratu*), both of which are spoken of as qualities worthy of sacrifice and propitiation (Yasna 22.29, 25.6; Yasht 2.1; Sirozah 1.2, 1.29, 2.2, 2.29). The illumination of the human mind comes through Vohu Manah. He is the presiding spirit of good thoughts and wisdom. Along with nobility of mind, he imparts enlightenment also. Both knowledge and wisdom are a means for his righteous acts. All devotees of Ahura Mazda receive Vohu Manah's power of wisdom and knowledge, which help to dispel the darkness of ignorance and its concomitant vices. Through Vohu Mana, the devout can aspire to reach Ahura Mazda (Yasna 36.4).

Moreover, those who marry and raise a family possess more of Vohu Manah than those who are celibate or ascetic (Vendidad 4.48). When the righteous cross the "great bridge" and come up to the gates of heaven, Vohu Manah rises from his golden throne situated at the right hand of Ahura Mazda and welcomes them to paradise (Vendidad 19.31–32). Those who do not seek Vohu Manah's counsel but indulge in wickedness are called the beloved of the demons, whose error will lead them to their just retribution (Yasna 32.4; 34.8–9). The wise, therefore, firmly resolve to embrace the divine precepts of Vohu Manah.

It is through Vohu Manah that Zoroaster, with hands uplifted in pious supplication, approaches Ahura Mazda (Yasna 28.2). He implores Ahura Mazda to grant him his heart's longing: the moment when, being enlightened and inspired, he may behold Vohu Manah (Yasna 28.5, 43.7–15). Ahura Mazda instructs Zoroaster to seek knowledge by day and by night to acquire the wisdom of Vohu Manah (Yasna 28.7–8; Yasht 1.20, 24.41; Vendidad 4.45, 18.6). Zoroaster further asks Ahura Mazda to grant the wishes of those who are worthy of Vohu Manah's reward (Yasna 28.10). In response, Ahura Mazda bestows the blessings of Vohu Manah on the faithful and righteous (Yasna 31.21, 43.2).

Vohu Manah's function in the material realm is the guardianship of the animal kingdom, the fifth of Ahura Mazda's creations. When Geush Urvan (the genius representing animal life) seeks a redress from the wrongs suffered by the kine at the hands of wicked herdsmen, Vohu Manah declares that Zoroaster is the man who by his teachings will inaugurate an era of human and animal prosperity (Yasna 29.7–8). Again, the diligent farmer who tends cattle is considered a promoter of Vohu Manah (Yasna 31.10, 47.3). Thus, in the spiritual sphere Vohu Manah personifies knowledge and wisdom, while in the physical realm he is the guardian spirit of animals.

Asha Vahishta

Asha Vahishta (or Asavahisht, Artavahisht, meaning "Best Righteousness") is the embodiment of divine law and moral order – the equivalent of righteousness (Yasna 31.8). Ahura Mazda is of one will with Asha Vahishta (Yasna 28.8, 29.7). This divine law of righteousness is more immutable than the heavens above and the earth below. The path of righteousness leads to the abode of Ahura Mazda, where Asha Vahishta dwells with other celestial beings in heaven (Yasna 30.10, 33.5; Yasht 3.3). Whereas the entire world of humanity gravitates toward Asha Vahishta, the world of divine beings lives in accordance with Asha Vahishta. No one besides Zoroaster undertook to establish the law of righteousness on earth among men and women (Yasna 29.8; Yasht 13.88). And by adopting Zoroaster's faith, King Vishtaspa helped to open the way for righteousness in the world (Yasht 13.99, 19.93).

Asha Vahishta co-operates with Ahura Mazda to bring about the final victory in this world, that of establishing the divine kingdom of righteousness (Yasht 47.6). The inauguration of the kingdom of righteousness is also hastened by the saintly actions of the righteous (*ashavan*), who possess the noblest moral character (Yasna 68.13, 72.11). To such persons, being religious is synonymous with Asha Vahishta. As a matter of fact, the word *asha* represents the highest value in Zoroastrian terminology. It is the norm by which the faithful guide their lives in this world, and the basis upon which the entire structure of the Zoroastrian faith rests.

Metaphysicians speculate about the origin of Asha Vahishta, and philosophers reflect; only the righteous imitate the actions of Asha Vahishta (Vendidad 10.19). The righteous attain greatness because they cultivate the friendship of Asha Vahishta and spread his divine law of righteousness throughout the world (Yasna 40.2). The highest value in human life is neither the attainment of happiness nor the achievement of peace but the incessant work of spreading the ideal of righteousness. To promote righteousness is to combat wickedness (Yasht 3.14–17).

In the realm of the material world, Asha Vahishta is the guardian spirit of fire (Yasht 17.20), the seventh of Ahura Mazda's creations. Fire, or light, is the most sacred emblem of purity in the Zoroastrian faith. Its presence serves as the visible symbol of Asha Vahishta (Yasna 34.4). And in the Zoroastrian liturgy Asha Vahishta is invoked together with fire (Yasna 1.4; Sirozah 1.7, 2.7). Thus, to meditate upon and pay homage to this concrete element of fire is tantamount to producing an offering to Ahura Mazda (Yasna 43.9).

Such identification in the realms of matter and spirit is brought into greater prominence in the Avestan text. Angra Mainyu (the Evil Spirit), for instance, exclaims that Zoroaster burns him through Asha Vahishta, as if with molten metal (Yasht 17.20). Thus, in the spiritual sphere Asha Vahishta personifies righteousness, while in the physical realm he is the protector of, and at times identified with, fire.

Khshathra Vairya

Khshathra Vairya (or Shahrevar, meaning "Desirable Kingdom," "Desirable Dominion") personifies Ahura Mazda's regal power of might, majesty, and sovereignty (Yasht 1.25). Ahura Mazda's divine kingdom is expressly that of Khshathra Vairya. Asha helps those who do what is right to attain Khshathra Vairya's goal: the establishment of the divine kingdom on earth (Yasna 51.1). The realization of this goal is dependent on the co-operation of human beings with Ahura Mazda. True, Ahura Mazda is the eternal sovereign of the universe, but his rule has been hampered by the Evil Spirit. To remove this imperfection, and to inaugurate his divine kingdom in which he shall rule supreme, Ahura Mazda requires the active participation of the righteous (Yasna 41.2).

Zoroaster laid the foundation of Khshathra Vairya by teaching humanity the virtue of obedience to the religion of Ahura Mazda (Yasna 33.14). Ever since, the pious pray and long for their share of enjoyment in the everlasting kingdom of Ahura Mazda (Yasna 41.2, 51.2), just as Zoroaster himself asked for the celestial riches and incomparable possessions of Khshathra Vairya (Yasna 33.13, 43.8).

In the realm of the material world, Khshathra Vairya guards the sky, the first of Ahura Mazda's creations; protects warriors; and presides over the metals that stand as his sign and symbol (Yasht 10.125; Vendidad 9.10, 16.6, 17.6). The final manifestation of Khshathra Vairya's desirable kingdom will be attended by the ordeal of molten metal, at which time the division between the righteous and the wicked will be evident (Yasna 30.7, 32.7, 51.9; Yasht 2.7; Visparad 20.1; Sirozah 1.4, 2.4). Thus, in the spiritual sphere Khshathra Vairya represents the celestial riches of the divine kingdom of Ahura Mazda, while in the physical realm he typifies the earthly riches embodied in the mineral world.

Spenta Armaiti

Spenta Armaiti (or Spendarmad, Asfandarmad, meaning "Holy Devotion", "Bountiful Devotion") is a feminine divine being, the daughter of Ahura Mazda and Heaven (Yasna 45.4). She personifies devotion, piety, religious harmony, and unswerving faith (Yasna 16.10; Vendidad 2.10–19). Spenta Armaiti gives the infallible ordinances of Ahura Mazda (Yasna 43.6). Indeed, she is Ahura Mazda's own beloved (Yasna 31.9) who will co-operate with him at the final dispensation (Yasna 47.6). Spenta Armaiti is the mother of Ashi Vanghuhi (genius of Good Piety), and is often invoked with Rata, the guardian spirit of generosity (Yasht 17.16; Sirozah 1.5, 2.5).

The faithful aspire to approach Ahura Mazda through the medium of Spenta Armaiti (Yasna 13.6, 39.5). The pious always choose to make her their own (Yasna 12.2). She is capable of protecting the faithful from malice and harm (Yasna 60.5; Yasht 1.28). Just as Vohu Manah enlightens the mind of the individual, so Armaiti purifies the heart of the pious (Yasna 48.5). Vohu Manah enlightens the mind to know Ahura Mazda; Spenta Armaiti inspires the heart to love God and lead a holy life (Yasna 51.21). The realization of Vohu Manah (Wisdom) and the devotion of Armaiti help the faithful to attain the ideal of Asha (Righteousness). Those who associate with evil estrange themselves from Spenta Armaiti and find themselves deserted by Asha (Yasna 34.9).

Zoroaster poured out his soul to Armaiti. He stated that he was the first and foremost devout person to venerate her ideals. He also inquired of her how he may spread Armaiti among those to whom he taught his faith (Yasna 44.11). He instructed the pious Frashaoshtra to follow the path of Asha and Armaiti (Yasna 48.11).

In the realm of the material world, Spenta Armaiti is the guardian spirit of the earth (Vendidad 3.35), the symbol of bountifulness and the third of Ahura Mazda's creations, as well as the protector of herdsmen and farmers. Frequently, however, she is spoken of as the earth itself rather than as the genius of the earth (Yasna 16.10; Yasht 24.50; Vendidad 2.10, 2.14, 2.18, 18.51, 18.64). Her garment is the star-studded sky. Thus, in the spiritual sphere Spenta Armaiti personifies the female spirit of devotion, while in the physical realm she represents, and later becomes, the earth.

Haurvatat and Ameretat

Haurvatat (or Xurdad, Hordad, meaning "Health," "Wholeness") is a feminine spirit who personifies complete health and perfection. Ameretat (or Amurdad, Murdad, meaning "Life," "Immortality") is also a feminine spirit who personifies immortality. Haurvatat and Ameretat are always mentioned together as the promised reward of the righteous after death in paradise (Yasna 1.2, 3.1, 4.1, 6.17, 7.26, 8.1, 34.11, 44.17, 45.5, 45.7, 45.10, 47.1, 58.7, 70.2, 71.12; Yasht 1.25,

10.92). Figuratively, Haurvatat and Ameretat represent the ambrosial food of the blessed in heaven, emblem of immortality (Yasna 34.11). Together they form a spiritual pair and share their sacred mantras, or formulas. Those who pronounce these mantras get the best rewards (Yasna 31.6).

Haurvatat and Ameretat were created by Ahura Mazda for the help, joy, comfort, and pleasure of the righteous (Yasht 4.1). The two together will smite the demons of hunger and thirst during the final conflict between the forces of good and evil (Yasht 19.96). Those who invoke the name of Haurvatat are able to smite a legion of demons (Yasht 4.2).

In the realm of the material world Haurvatat is the guardian spirit of water, the second of Ahura Mazda's creations. Ameretat presides over vegetation, the fourth of Ahura Mazda's creations. Thus, Haurvatat and Ameretat form a spiritual pair indissolubly bound together for the welfare of humanity, representing perfection and immortality. And on the physical side these dual spirits represent water and vegetation, which have a healing effect on human beings (Yasht 19.96).

Homage to Amesha Spenta

These six Amesha Spenta surround the throne of Ahura Mazda and dwell in the unseen world. They sit upon thrones of gold in paradise (Vendidad 19.32) and descend on paths of light (Yasht 3.1, 13.84, 19.17) to receive the special oblation offered them by pious adherents of the Zoroastrian faith during the ritual worship dedicated to them.

Each Amesha Spenta fills a prominent place in the Zoroastrian faith; each has a special month assigned to his or her honour (Bundahishn 25.20); each has also a special day as a holy day; and each has a particular flower as an appropriate emblem (Bundahishn 27.24). Along with Ahura Mazda, the Amesha Spenta are to be propitiated and honoured by the faithful (Yasht 19.14–20; Visparad 19.1–2; Shayest ne-Shayest 15.4–31). The existence and propitiation of the Amesha Spenta is a characteristic feature of the Zoroastrian faith which probably originated with Zoroaster himself (Yasna 30.9, 31.4).

YAZATA

Next in rank to the Amesha Spenta, Zoroastrians recognize a group of minor spirits or divinities (sometimes thought of as angels) called

Yazata (or Yazad, Izad, Fereshte, meaning "Adorable Ones," "Worshipful Beings"), who carry out still further the will of Ahura Mazda. Their number is, theoretically, legion (Yasht 6.1; Visparad 8.1) but the extant Avesta mentions only some forty names.

Two groups of Yazata may be distinguished in the Avesta: Indo-Iranian (i.e., common to Indians and Iranians), and Iranian. Those that are common to both Indians and Iranians include Mithra, Vayu, Verethraghna, Rata, Airyaman, Haoma, Parendi, and Ushah. Those that are purely Iranian are Atar, Ardvi Sura Anahita, Tishtrya, Sraosha, Rashnu, Daena, Christi, Ashi Vanghuhi, Asman, Zamyat, and many more. Some Yazata mentioned in the Avesta do not appear in the Gathas; others are so prominent that they have a Yasht (hymn or praise) consecrated to them individually (Yasht 3, 5, 6, 7, 9, 14, 17, 54, 57). Ahura Mazda stands, naturally, at the head of the Yazata. In fact, he is called the greatest and the best of the Yazata (Yasna 16.1; Yasht 17.16). Even Zoroaster is called, at least once, a Yazata (Yasna 3.21).

The Yazata include both genders and represent abstract ideas or virtues as well as concrete objects of nature. Two distinct orders may be recognized in the Avesta: celestial or spiritual (*mainyava*) and terrestrial or material (*gaethya*), though no indication is given as to where any particular Yazata belongs (Yasna 1.19, 3.4, 7.4, 16.9, 22.27, 25.8, 71.5; Yasht 6.4, 19.22). Many of them are said to preside over both the spiritual sphere and material phenomena. Often the names of the Yazata designate merely the objects of nature that they personify. Sometimes, praise and sacrifice are offered more to the concrete objects of nature than to the Yazata presiding over each object. This dual aspect of the Yazata makes it difficult to distinguish the Yazata from the personified object; some lack any real character.

No distinction is made between the genders. Both occupy the same place of honour, receive the same degree of homage, and are on the same level in inspiring awe or manifesting power. Some of the Yazata act as the guardian spirit for more than one abstract virtue and impersonate more than one natural phenomenon. It is not uncommon to find one Yazata sharing the characteristic qualities and functions of another. Sometimes one Yazata enters into partnership with various other Yazata, according to the nature of the sphere of activity.

One of the major functions of the Yazata is to help and grant various blessings to those who invoke them with offerings and sacrifices (Yasna 65.12, 65.14). They are said to gather together by the hundreds and thousands to pour upon the earth the light of the sun (Yasht 6.1). They protect and help individuals during war or peace, provided that these individuals propitiate them with praise, invocation, and offerings. The usual manner of propitiating the Yazata is to invoke each one separately by name, or in pairs, or in the company of his or her associates. Sometimes all the Yazata are invoked collectively under the comprehensive title of "all Yazata" (*vispe Yazata*; Yasna 1.19, 2.18; Yasht 11.17, 17.19). And, in fact, the entire book of the Visparat, literally meaning "all lords," is dedicated to numerous Yazata. In actual practice, the principal Yazata (Yasna 16.3–16) seem to be those to whom a day in the month is assigned as a holy day, or to whom a special season is consecrated with a form of ritual worship.

Apart from the collective service they perform, each Yazata personifies a number of divine attributes and presides over one or more of Ahura Mazda's creations. A few examples will suffice to illustrate this. The male Yazata Atar (Fire) is called the "son" of Ahura Mazda and represents the splendour and majesty of priests and kings. The female Yazata Ashi (Piety) is offended when maidens remain unmarried and chastises those who either vitiate the law of chastity or sell their bodies for profit. The male Yazata Sraosha (Hear, Obey) is the protector of the righteous, watches over all creatures, and oversees human souls.

In addition, a large number of them are personifications of virtues or noble traits, such as Hvaranah (Glory) and Cista (Reason). Others represent celestial constellations, such as Tistar (or Tistrya), Satavaesa, Vanad (or Vanat), and Airyaman Isya (Yasht 8.20). This latter Yazata is invoked in connection with wedding rites, and is often considered the healer of diseases whose help is invoked for warding off demons and death (Videvdat 20.10–12).

FRAVASHI

The Fravashi (or Fravarti, Fravahar, Fraohar) are conscious beings who existed with Ahura Mazda long before the creation of the universe. They are the perfect types of imperfect objects in the world. In other words, they are the celestial originals of terrestrial duplicates – the double of every heavenly and earthly being or element. Even Ahura Mazda, the Amesha Spenta, and the Yazata all have their personal Fravashi (Yasna 23.2; Yasht 13.80, 13.82, 13.85). But so does every individual, and sky, earth, water, plants, animals, and all objects created by Ahura Mazda (Yasht 13.74, 13.76). Thus, every entity or element, from the highest divine being to the tiniest object on earth, is endowed with a Fravashi. Only Ahriman, his demons, and all objects that are evil by nature are without a Fravashi.

The Fravashi help both divine and human beings by warning and guarding against evil, and by promoting all that is useful and advantageous (Bundahishn 2.10; Denkard 8.7.11–13). Like the Amesha Spenta and the Yazata, the Fravashi are allotted their respective tasks by Ahura Mazda. Through them, Ahura Mazda maintains the heavens and the earth (Yasht 13.1, 13.2, 13.9, 13.22, 13.28, 13.29). Ninety-nine thousand nine hundred and ninety-nine Fravashi watch over Zoroaster's seed, which will give birth to three saviours in the last tri-millennium phase of this world (Bundahishn 32.8–9; see below for more discussion).

The longest Yasht in the Avesta (Yasht 13) is totally dedicated to the praise of the Fravashi. They are usually designated as the most powerful, the most mighty, the most valiant, the most holy, and the most effective. They move swiftly to grant victory, health, and glory to those who invoke their name. Although beneficent by nature, they are quite efficacious in disarming tyrants and enemies. Their power and efficiency are beyond description and cannot be conceived by the mind. Waters, plants, trees, wind, sun, moon, and stars all owe their movements to the influence of the Fravashi. Women conceive offspring and have easy childbirth through the radiance and glory of the Fravashi. Moreover, children destined to fame and honour attain this distinction thanks to the Fravashi. In fact, were it not for their guardianship, all life, including animal and human, would cease to exist because Ahriman would destroy it forever.

Nothing is mentioned about the gradation in rank or the differences in gender of the Fravashi. What is stated clearly, however, is that those who piously solicit their goodwill and propitiate them with offerings receive the very best of blessings from the spiritual world. But those who neglect or offend them receive the curse of untold harm (Yasht 13.30–31, 13.51–52). Hence, the righteous honour the Fravashi with prayers and offerings in the hope that their supplication will be transmitted to Ahura Mazda and to the Amesha Spenta (Yasht 13.156–7).

Each individual possesses a Fravashi from the moment of birth right through till death. This Fravashi is the higher double of the individual and acts as a divine voice, a guardian spirit, and a true guiding friend. It remains unaffected and untouched (i.e., pure and sinless) by an individual's thoughts, words, or actions. Throughout the individual's span of life, it warns, admonishes, protects, applauds, criticizes, counsels, and threatens, according to the situation at hand. Nonetheless, the individual alone is responsible for the good or evil done in this world, with its concomitant reward or punishment in the next.

At death, the Fravashi of the individual returns to the celestial realm to live as an individualized Fravashi of that person. Such Fravashi long to communicate with the living, among whom they lived on earth. Hence, special days are set apart for that purpose, when the descendants of the deceased invoke the Fravashi of the dead by offerings and prayer, and by soliciting their help and favour. So, the nineteenth day of every month of the Zoroastrian calendar is consecrated to the memory of the Fravashi of the dead; the last ten days of the year, including the five intercalary days, are specially set apart for their ritual worship; and the first month of the Zoroastrian calendar receives its name from them.

In addition, it is the sacred duty of the faithful to perform the rites of commemoration of the Fravashi on the anniversaries of the deceased. The performance of such rites by the descendants of the deceased is believed to enable the soul of the deceased in the next world to progress from a lower to a higher state. If the living descendants neglect to perform these duties and fail to offer their prayer and sacrifice to the Fravashi of the dead, then on the day when they approach the next world they can expect only the reproach and curses of these Fravashi.

AHRIMAN

In contrast to all these divine forces created by Ahura Mazda to represent the principles of goodness are the forces created by Ahriman to represent the principles of evil. Evil, in the Zoroastrian faith, is considered to have as independent and complete an existence as good. Both exist entirely separate from each other and are primeval. Neither good originates from evil, nor evil from good. The fundamental purpose of all human beings is to maintain the well-being of the created order of Ahura Mazda. He is absolutely good and, therefore, cannot be considered the creator of any kind of evil, natural or moral. All the evil in the world is the creative work of Ahriman.[3]

Ahriman, then, is considered to be the inveterate foe of the supreme God, Ahura Mazda, and the origin of all suffering, affliction, bodily deformities, evil, and death (Yasna 29.1, 30.4, 30.6, 31.3; Videvdat 2.29, 2.37, 20.3, 22.2). His place was originally in the pit of endless darkness (Bundahishn 1.39; Zadspram 1.17; Dadastan i Dinig 37.28), but in the beginning of Ahura Mazda's creation he rushed upon the entire world to bring harm and destruction (Bundahishn 3.11, 3.14, 6.1; Zadspram 2.3). For every one of Ahura Mazda's benevolent spiritual powers, Ahriman conjured up an opposing malevolent creature of equivalent rank and power as aides to counterbalance every good creation of Ahura Mazda with an evil one of his own. Thus, the phenomenal world consists of pairs of conflicting opposites: light/dark, truth/falsehood, health/sickness, rain/drought, pure/impure, good creatures/noxious creatures, life/death, heaven/hell.

Because Ahriman is not omniscient (Bundahishn 1.16), he cannot foresee his own final defeat. And since he is an after-thinker, he knows nothing of events to come (Denkard, SAN vol. 4, p. 258). He is stupid, ill-informed, totally ignorant, and blind (Bundahishn 1.19). He was not even aware of the existence of Ahura Mazda until he arose from his eternal place in the abyss.

Ahriman prompts all human beings to perform evil deeds and instigates discord, violence, and licentiousness (Bundahishn 3.17; Dadastan i Dinig 37.8; Menog i Xrad 45.8). He deceives human beings and obstructs them from hearing and accepting the message of Ahura Mazda (Bundahishn 1.8, 1.10, 28.1–6). He is a father of lies, a murderer from the beginning, and the source of death (Bundahishn 3.17; Dadastan i Dinig 37.46, 37.72, 37.81–82). He is an oppressor of mankind's happiness as well as the inveterate enemy of Ahura Mazda (Bundahishn 3.15, 3.24; Zadspram 4.3, 4.10). He rules over a large host of evil spirits that will all be defeated eventually in a decisive combat.

One of Ahriman's many malicious acts was to infest the earth with noxious creatures, such as snakes, scorpions, lizards, frogs, and many others (Bundahishn 3.15; Zadspram 2.9). Hence, killing these noxious creatures is considered by Zoroastrians a meritorious deed. Again, Ahriman introduced evil into vegetation by producing weeds, thorns, poison ivy, and many other harmful elements of nature (Bundahishn 3.16, 3.24, 27.1; Zadspram 2.11). But little does he realize that his evil existence will cease at the hands of Ahura Mazda when the end of his allotted time arrives (Bundahishn 1.3).

ANGRA MAINYU

The arch-enemy on earth to Spenta Mainyu and the agent through whom Ahriman works is Angra Mainyu (Hostile Spirit, Evil Spirit; Yasna 57.17; Yasht 11.12, 13.76, 15.3, 15.43–44). He is considered the demon of demons, a tyrant, doer of evil deeds, inveterately wicked, and the one who introduces discord and death (Yasna 27.1, 30.4, 61.2; Yasht 3.13, 10.97, 10.118, 13.71, 13.78, 19.97; Vendidad 19.1, 19.3, 19.43). He infects the bodies of mortals with deformities, disease, and decay (Vendidad 2.29, 2.37, 20.3, 22.2). He corrupts the moral nature of human beings by his malicious thoughts and teachings and incites them to rebel against the divine authority of Ahura Mazda (Yasna 19.15).

The demons (*daeva*) have struck an allegiance with Angra Mainyu to mar the "good creation" of Ahura Mazda (Yasna 30.6). As Angra Mainyu's associates, the demons spread their mischief throughout the world and lead human beings away from the path of "the good religion." However, the recital of the Ahuna Vairya prayer puts Angra Mainyu to flight, just as it did when Ahura Mazda recited it at the beginning of creation (Yasna 19.15).

As the counterpart of Spenta Mainyu, Angra Mainyu exists from the beginning (Yasna 30.3–4, 45.2). He is surrounded by demons in the kingdom of night and darkness (Yasna 30.6) and stands at the opposite pole to Spenta Mainyu (Yasna 45.2). The north is his seat, or rather, the place where he fosters evil to attack the world of righteousness (Vendidad 19.1, 44). For every good creation of Ahura Mazda, Angra Mainyu counter-created an evil one. Thus, a constant war has been waged ever since he first struck the world of righteousness (Yasht 13.77). But in the end, righteousness will triumph over wickedness, and Angra Mainyu will be forced to his eternal destiny of doom (Yasht 19.96).

ARCHDEMONS

Just as there are six Amesha Spenta, so are there six archdemons (seven, if Ahriman is included) who fight constantly with the six Holy Immortals (Bundahishn 1.24, 1.27, 30.29; Videvdat 10.9, 19.43, 19.49). The following diagram illustrates this cosmic forces of opposition:

Benevolent Powers	Malevolent Powers
Ahura Mazda	Ahriman
Vohu Manah	Aka Manah
Asha Vahishta	Indra
Khshathra Vairya	Saura
Spenta Armaiti	Naonghaithya
Haurvatat and Ameretat	Taurvi and Zairich

Ahriman produced each of these six archdemons in exact opposition to Amesha Spenta for their diabolical work in disrupting the entire plan of Ahura Mazda (Dadastan i Dinig 37.59). Their strongest weapon against humanity is deceit or falsehood. Those who associate with these demons in this world deserve to have demons for their companions in the next.

Aka Manah (or Akoman) occupies the first place among evil creatures after Angra Mainyu. His activity is in direct opposition to Vohu Manah (Bundahishn 1.27). He perverts the mind of human beings with evil thoughts and blunts their intelligence. He is said to bring evil knowledge of religion, as opposed to "the good religion," and cause human discord and spiritual disruption. The reason why children cry at birth is because Aka Manah is said to frighten them with ghastly pictures of their suffering on the Day of Renovation (Denkard, SAN vol. 8, p. 439).

The chief business of Indra (or Indar) is to drive away human thoughts from virtuous deeds and to incite individuals to cease to wear the sacred shirt and thread – symbols of the Zoroastrian faith (Bundahishn 28.8). Saura (or Sovar), too, is delighted if the faithful discard the sacred symbols of the Zoroastrian faith (Bundahishn 28.10). But Saura's main activity is to introduce tyranny and anarchy in the world in order to disrupt the work of Khshatra Vairya, the divine kingdom of righteousness (Bundahishn 28.9).

Naonghaithya (or Naonghas), who is identified with the demon Taromat, dries up the spring of devotion in human beings, produces disobedience, and dissuades individuals from following the dictates of Spenta Mainyu (Bundahishn 28.14; Dadastan i Dinig 94.2). Taurvi (or Tairev) and Zairich (or Zairicha) are opponents of Haurvatat and Ameretat respectively. As such, they cause imperfection and mortality and poison plants and all other edible products (Bundahishn 28.11; Dadastan i Dinig 37.52). Little do these archdemons know, however, that they will be routed in the end by their counterparts and totally perish in the final conflagration (Bundahishn 30.29).

DEMONS

Opposing the Yazata are the demons (*daeva*) or evil spirits, whose number are legion, though the Avesta mentions only about forty-five by name (Yasna 27.1, 57.17; Yasht 9.4, 19.18; Bundahishn 28.12, 28.14–46; Vendidad 10.16). These hordes of evil spirits are poorly depicted in the Zoroastrian scriptures. In many cases their traits appear blurred, though on the whole they seem to be diabolic, of fiendish character, and the embodiment of all that is evil (Yasht 10.50, 13.57; Vendidad 18.54–55, 19.3). They are of both genders and their motive is to assault, to create trouble, to plot against, to bewitch, to seduce, to destroy, and to kill all human beings while they are in this world, and to torment the souls of the wicked after death.

All demons are instigators of some evil. Consequently, they should be abjured and relentlessly put down (Yasna 34.5). All heretics and rebels to "the good religion" are called *daevayasna* (worshippers of the demons), as distinguished from the *mazdayasna* (worshippers of Mazda). When the righteous shall triumph at last, when humanity shall reach perfection at the final restoration, then all the demons, including the archdemons and Ahriman, will sink to their original pit of darkness and perish forever (Dadastan i Dinig 37.20).

COSMIC DUALISM

The Zoroastrian concept of dualism, as noted above, is not the metaphysical dualism of spirit and matter that the Pythagorean and Orphic religions taught, and Plato and other philosophers believed. It is the dualism of two opposing, personified forces in the universe, a good God and an evil adversary. This type of thinking may be described as cosmic dualism, since the entire cosmos, heaven, earth, and the underworld, along with their inhabitants, are involved in the opposition between the powers of good and evil.

Ahura Mazda personifies the principle and source of all good: success, glory, honour, physical health, and immortality. Ahriman embodies the principle and source of all evil: misfortune, disaster, war, sickness, and death. Ahura Mazda created heaven, earth, and mankind. Moreover, he represents light, truth, justice, and life. Ahriman is the originator and initiator of all evil. He represents darkness, falsehood, injustice, and the absence of life (Yasna 29.1, 30.4, 30.6; Videvdat 2.29, 2.37, 20.3, 22.2).

The struggle of Ahura Mazda and Ahriman in Zoroastrian teaching extends over the entire seen and unseen world. This world is a great battlefield in which the beneficent powers of Ahura Mazda ceaselessly contend with the baleful forces of Ahriman. Light struggles with darkness, the vivifying waters with drought and barrenness, warmth with icy conditions, useful animals with beasts of prey, industrious peasants and herdsmen with marauding nomads, civilized people with barbarians; the destructive forces both in nature and in society are not guided by chance or blind laws, but by the warring of benevolent and malevolent powers.

To Zoroastrians, therefore, the universe is an eternal battleground where a pair of coexistent, divine, and warring principles combat. In every sphere and in every situation demanding a decision between two opposites, human beings have to make a choice between these two principles. The consequences alone imply that the principle of good is more powerful than the principle of evil, and that therefore Ahura Mazda eventually triumphs.

Thus, Zoroastrian teaching depicts Ahura Mazda and Ahriman as two adversaries having contrary and incompatible natures. They seem to have existed in this state from the beginning, since the question of their origin is not raised (Yasna 30.3, 45.2).[4] What is emphatically stated, however, is that good is good and evil is evil, and it is impossible for the one to proceed from the other. To deny the existence of a separate principle of evil is unthinkable in Zoroastrian belief, because it is tantamount to imputing evil to Ahura Mazda.

If Ahura Mazda is good, then he cannot produce evil; if he is perfect, then nothing can be added to him. All the evil and injury in this universe is caused by Ahriman. How can one conceive of Ahura Mazda as an omnipotent and wholly perfect god if Ahriman is responsible for evil and can invade and hold sway over the creation of Ahura Mazda? The answer lies in the limitation of the power of Ahriman and the triumph of Ahura Mazda in the end. Ahriman is never equal to Ahura Mazda. He is handicapped by possessing "backward knowledge." He cannot foresee what Ahura Mazda invents; all he can do is to set up an opposed power, a means of attack. Hence, Ahriman is limited in power, knowledge, and time, and ultimately doomed to defeat.

ZURVAN

This fundamental principle of cosmic dualism did not go unchallenged. A heterodox group called the Zurvanites tried to establish a unified godhead based on an exegesis of Yasna 30.2 and 30.3, whereby Ahura Mazda and Ahriman were seen as twin sons of Zurvan-i-akanarak (or Zrvan-akarana, Infinite Time; a minor divinity of late Younger Avestan texts). The heresy may have been adopted as orthodoxy by some Achaemenian, and later Sasanid, kings, but the rigorous reaction of the orthodox Zoroastrians brought the heresy to an end by the tenth century CE, and every effort was made to expunge from Zoroastrian texts all traces of Zurvanite ideas. Nevertheless, Zurvanite teachings may be pieced together from Zoroastrian as well as from Christian, Manichaean, and Islamic sources, though the information provided in these non-Zoroastrian sources is unsympathetic and even hostile.[5]

In a very interesting passage, for instance, Yeghisheh, the Armenian Christian historian of the fifth century CE, presents the Zurvanite concept of dualism: the origin of good and evil. This concept was postulated on the belief in an incessant strife waged between two primary entities, Ohrmazd (Ahura Mazda), the Good, and Ahriman, the Evil, who were begotten by a divine primordial being, Zurvan. Zurvan, according to Yeghisheh, wanted a son, and to this end he offered sacrifices. After some time he was seized with doubts and wondered whether he would have any offspring, but soon he conceived twins.

The first of the twins, whom Zurvan named Ahriman, was black and evil-smelling. The second was Ohrmazd. These twins had to choose between good and evil. Ahriman chose evil while Ohrmazd chose good. This is Yeghisheh's description:

Before there existed heaven and earth, the great god Zurvan offered sacrifices for a thousand years and said: "Perhaps I will have a son by the name of Ohrmazd who will create heaven and earth." And he conceived two in his womb, one for offering sacrifice and the other for saying "perhaps." When he perceived that there were two in his womb, he said: "Whoever comes first, to him will I give my sovereignty." But he who had been conceived in doubt ruptured the womb and came out. Zurvan said to him: "Who are you?" "I am your son Ohrmazd," said he. Zurvan said to him: "My son is radiant and fragrant, you are dark and wicked." And when he [the son] cried bitterly, he [Zurvan] gave him the sovereignty for a thousand years. When the other son was also born, he named him Ohrmazd. He took the sovereignty from Ahriman and gave it to Ohrmazd and said to him: "Up to now I sacrificed to you, and now you sacrifice to me."

And Ohrmazd created heaven and earth, while Ahriman opposed him and did evil. Hence, all creatures were thus divided: the angels belong to Ohrmazd, while the devils to Ahriman. And all the good which comes from heaven to earth belongs to Ohrmazd, while whatever evil is performed here and there, belongs to Ahriman. Similarly, whatever is evil has been created by Ahriman. For example, Ohrmazd created man, while diseases, sicknesses and death have been created by Ahriman. And all misfortunes, disasters and bitter wars are the work of the evil principle; while success, sovereignty, glory, honour and physical health, as well as beauty of countenance, eloquence of speech, and longevity owe their existence to the good principle.[6]

Such alien ideas concerning the origin of cosmic dualism were rigorously excluded from orthodox Zoroastrian teachings. Consequently, the concept of Zurvan does not apply to modern Zoroastrian theology. What is stressed instead is the relation between the doctrine of cosmic dualism and the principle of the freedom of human choice, together with the law of consequences.

HUMAN CHOICE

The implication of this cosmic dualism is that human beings, according to Zoroastrian teaching, are not merely passive spectators of the war between Ahura Mazda's and Ahriman's host of allies, on which their fortunes and their very existence depend. Every individual is, by her and his own choice, engaged in this cosmic warfare, contending for the defeat of Ahriman and the ultimate triumph of Ahura Mazda. The whole conflict is therefore a war of moral choices: right or wrong, truth or falsehood, justice or injustice. In one sense, then, human life is regarded as a war, or personal defence, against evil spirits. Those persons who pray to Ahura Mazda daily and live a pious life; who are humble, patient, truth-speakers, and pure of heart; who possess virtues and good characteristics; and who avoid wrath, greediness, jealousy, enmity, lying, stealing, laziness, and asceticism, establish the proper relationship with the spiritual powers and maintain the purity and well-being of the created order of Ahura Mazda. Asceticism, renunciation, celibacy, and fasting have no place in Zoroastrian teaching.

This means that the whole human drama – indeed, the ultimate purpose of existence – is reduced to just one element: choice. Every person is genuinely free to pursue either of two paths: good and evil. One's choice here and now determines one's eternal destiny.

This freedom to choose between good and evil, and the inevitable consequences of such a choice, evolve from a moral triad and its evil opposite: purity of thought (*humata*), word (*hukta*) and deed (*huvarashta*); or impurity of thought (*dushmata*), word (*duzukhta*), and deed (*duzvarshta*). This triad is, in turn, an inseparable component of the three elements that constitute the greatest gifts of Ahura Mazda to mankind: body, soul, and mind. The most precious of these three is the mind – the faculty that distinguishes right from wrong, pure from impure, truth from falsehood, good from evil. Consequently, there is no recourse to atonement or intercession and no provision for them. Eternal salvation rests on the efficacy of one's own good thoughts, good words, and good deeds.[7]

The practical nature of Zoroastrian teaching is quite obvious. Metaphysical issues and speculative thought have little, if any, part in Zoroastrian teaching. Human salvation is constituted on the full realization of life, not the negation of it. The duty of each individual is to side with the good so that the evil will be ultimately vanquished and the good will triumph to reign supreme.

BEYOND DEATH

The sum and substance of this moral triad determines also the fate of every individual after death. At death, the soul of an individual stays with the body for three days (Yasht 22.1–6, 22.19–24, 24.54;

Videvdat 19.27–29; Dadastan i Dinig 28.5). On the fourth day, the soul journeys to the place of judgment by crossing the "Chinvat Bridge" (possibly a ford over an underground river, guarded by supernatural dogs), which spans the abyss of hell and leads to paradise on the other side (Yasht 3.4; Bundahishn 12.7; 19.36). If the record of that soul's life on earth is represented in the balance by a weighty accumulation of good thoughts, words, and deeds, then the soul meets its own conscience in the shape of a "fair maiden" and crosses without difficulty to paradise. But if the reverse is the case, then the passage over the Chinvat Bridge becomes an entirely different experience for the soul. The bridge turns on its side, presenting a knife's edge footing like the edge of a sword, and the soul perceives its own conscience in the shape of an "ugly hag" and plunges into the abyss of hell (Dadastan i Dinig 21.3, 21.5, 21.7, 25.6, 34.3–4, 85.7).

While paradise is a place of beauty, light, pleasant scents, and bliss, to be enjoyed by those who adhere in life to the Zoroastrian moral and ceremonial teachings (Yasna 30.11; 43.5; 45.7), hell is a place of horror, misery, darkness, evil smells, and suffering for those who violate in life the same Zoroastrian teachings (Yasht 22, 24; Bundahishn 13, 28, 30; Arda Wiraz Namag 27, 28, 29, 36, 38, 48, 49). If the good and evil deeds done in life exactly balance, then the soul remains in an intermediate place called *hamestagan* (or *hamestagna*, *hamestakan*; the Purgatory of Christianity) until the day of resurrection and final judgment. Here the soul suffers no torment except the seasonal temperature of heat and cold (Yasht 22; Dadastan i Dinig 27.2). This "limbo" state is conceived to be located in the region between heaven and earth, and the place is of considerable discomfort but imposes no intense torture.

DISPENSATION

The bliss of souls in heaven and the torment of those in hell is not regarded as a final state. When the appointed time arrives, three saviours will appear, at intervals of a millennium, to herald the Messianic Age (Menog i Xrad 2.95). These three saviours will bring to completion and perfection the work of reclaiming humanity from evil, and they will regenerate the universe. Thus, the concepts of time and beyond-time, including certain distinct periods that separate the ages (past, present, and future), are of prime importance in Zoroastrian teaching.

There are four tri-millennium periods of time (Bundahishn 1). During the first tri-millennium, the primary ideas of all good creations remained motionless and insensible. At the close of this first period, however, Ahriman saw a gleam of light while wandering near·the upper bounds of the dark domain. Consequently, he conceived the desire to seize the celestial realm and to control the entire universe. In order to accomplish this purpose, he created a vast army of fiends, demons, wizards, and all sorts of eternally evil, noxious creatures (Bundahishn 3.1–17; Zadspram 2).

Unprepared to withstand such an attack, Ahura Mazda concluded a treaty with Ahriman for three more tri-millennium periods. This treaty specified that the world would first be ruled by Ahura Mazda for three thousand years, then by Ahriman for the same period. During the last three thousand years the two antagonists would strive for mastery.

Because of his omniscience, Ahura Mazda was able to outwit Ahriman during his tri-millennium period. He created the primeval ox and the primeval man, representing the animal kingdom and the human race respectively. Furthermore, to insure his own ultimate victory, he caused the spiritual body of Zoroaster to be fashioned, knowing that Zoroaster would one day be incarnated as the instrument by which Ahriman was to be ultimately destroyed.

When Ahriman's turn arrived to rule, he proceeded to disrupt the entire creation. He corrupted the earth by mixing smoke with fire, sowing thorns, destroying vegetation, and creating billions of noxious creatures and destructive beasts. Nature itself served his evil purpose and generated storms, droughts, and earthquakes.

Moreover, Ahriman dug a great hole in the earth to be the infernal region. He debased all mankind by filling them with corrupt words, wicked thoughts, and evil desires. And he destined the human race to suffering, misery, and total annihilation in the everlasting fires of hell. Fortunately, however, his period of rule was to end before he could succeed in his final plan of extirpating mankind.

Thirty years before the beginning of the final tri-millennium phase (in the year 8970 according to the Zoroastrian calendar, or 660 BCE by western reckoning), Ahura Mazda sent Zoroaster into the world. Hence, the final tri-millennium period began with the ministry of the prophet Zoroaster, when he was thirty years old (in 630 BCE). His mission was to teach humanity "the good religion" and reveal to them the great events that would happen during this last period.

APPEARANCE OF SAVIOURS

The prophecies of Zoroaster, revealing the word of Ahura Mazda, indicate that at the close of each millennium a great saviour will appear in order to reconstitute "the good religion" (Bundahishn 30, 32.5–9). Each of these three saviours – namely, Hushedar, Aushedar-Mah, and Saoshyant (Yasht 13.128, 13.141–142; Videvdat 19.5; Menog i Xrad 2.95) – will be a direct descendant of Zoroaster (whose seed is preserved in a lake) and born through a virgin birth (by a mother who will go to bathe in the lake; Bundahishn 32.8, 33.36–38, 35.56–60). Each will be attended with portents and miraculous signs.

The appearance of Hushedar will be preceded by successively degenerating regimes. All people will become deceivers and affection will depart from the world; brothers, even father and son, will hate each other. All the sacred rites and ceremonies will be treated with contempt. Wrath and avarice will precede total apostasy. Then, in those horrible days, the sun and the moon will show signs; there will be frightful earthquakes and terrible storms. Wars and battles will greatly increase and many soldiers will be slain (Yasht 1, 2.15–37, 3.4–44).

But from the moment of the appearance of the first saviour to the end of the period of the last saviour, righteousness will prevail more and more in the world. Before the arrival of the day of resurrection of the dead and of the renovation of the universe, the ideal teachings of Zoroaster, or rather, "the good religion" of Ahura Mazda, will be spread to the ends of the world. All evil and wickedness will perish, because the entire human race will embrace righteousness by practising "the good religion" (Yasna 45.11; Bundahishn 30.17–33). All those who happen to be living at that time will join the ranks of those resurrected from the dead.

RESURRECTION AND JUDGMENT

When the appointed time arrives, all the dead, righteous and wicked alike, will arise on the spot where they died (Bundahishn 30.7). Thus, earth and sea will surrender their dead and all will be gathered before the judgment seat (Yasht 3.18–21, 3.56–58; Bundahishn 30). The souls of both the righteous and the wicked will be reunited with their bodies – the bones being demanded back from the earth, the blood from water, the hair from plants, and the life from fire – so that they are reconstituted once again in their original materials (Bundahishn 30.6). Then, these reconstituted individuals will assemble in one place and know of each other's deeds performed on earth (Bundahishn 30.10). Next, the righteous and the wicked will be separated from each other and sent in their reconstituted form to heaven or hell for three days. The wicked will be cast into the depths of hell, where frightful punishments, torture, filth, and darkness will be their share. The righteous, on the other hand, will enter heaven and enjoy every imaginable bliss in the realm of endless light. And all those in whom good and evil do not outweigh each other but balance will remain in the intermediary place called *hamestagan*.

Three days later, both the righteous and the wicked will be purified by walking through a molten metal (Yasna 32.7, 51.9). Now, all will speak in one tongue and proclaim their praise to Ahura Mazda and his entities. Then an ambrosia of immortality will be given to all. As a result, adults will be restored as men and women of forty, children as youths of fifteen. Life will be restored back to its pristine state, with each man having his wife, and offspring without procreation.

RENOVATION OF THE UNIVERSE

In the meantime, Ahriman will be able to mobilize a vast army for the great and final Armageddon battle. There will be so much slaughter that the rivers of blood will reach the girths of the horses. Nevertheless, the result will be the ultimate triumph of Ahura Mazda. Then there will come the great conflagration in which the world will burn in a fantastic holocaust. Ahriman and all his followers, including the inhabitants of the pit of hell, will be burned and annihilated. Everything will be destroyed and a new universe will come into being. Finally, there will follow an eternity of bliss, and the will of Ahura Mazda will prevail supreme.[8]

QUESTION OF INFLUENCE

It is impossible to write about Zoroastrian teachings without commenting on the possible Zoroastrian influence on Judaism, Christianity, and Islam (and vice versa). The striking resemblances (and differences) between some characteristic Zoroastrian teachings and practices and those of Judaism, Christianity, and Islam have certainly attracted the attention of both biblical and Iranian specialists.[9] Two extreme positions have emerged in the course of scholarly discussions.[10] One insists that Zoroastrian ideas and tenets greatly influenced not only Judaism but Christianity and Islam as well.[11] The other diametrically opposes this view, and even maintains that influence moved in the opposite direction, that is, from Judaism to Zoroastrianism.[12]

Needless to say, the controversy stems from the absence of concrete, positive evidence, which creates considerable difficulties in tracing with precision or certainty the question of exchange of religious ideas and practices. And to make matters worse, the difficulties inherent in the Iranian literature present problems of interpretation. The group of hymns known as the Gathas are quite commonly accepted to be the earliest layer of Zoroastrian religious literature, possibly composed by Zoroaster himself. But, as stated in an earlier chapter, there is no unanimous agreement either on the date of Zoroaster or on the interpretation of the content of his composition. Some scholars, therefore, tend to ignore the Zoroastrian tradition of exegesis altogether and attempt to reconstruct the meaning of the Gathas by a close study with the literature of India, primarily the existing literary monument known as the Rig-veda. Others give a great deal of credence to later Zoroastrian tradition, in spite of its divergence from the original Zoroastrian teachings.

Subsequent portions of the Avesta dealing with questions of doctrine, cosmology, cosmogony, and eschatology are also not free from textual difficulties and corruption. In addition, the final redaction of the literature preserved in Pahlavi seems to derive from the centuries following the Muslim Arab conquest of Iran in the seventh century CE. This raises an important question: did the Zoroastrian interpreters of that period read into these texts ideas that belonged to their period rather than the period in which the ancient tradition was first formulated? The available evidence is of little help. Thus, the lack of firm, positive evidence, placed in its proper historical setting, by which to evaluate the Zoroastrian influence on Judaism, Christianity, and Islam has led some scholars to view this field of discussion with suspicion.

It is, of course, common knowledge that the Jewish people came into close contact with Zoroastrianism during their exile in Babylon in the sixth century BCE. This period of Jewish-Persian contact (particularly in the sixth to fourth centuries BCE) was in many ways decisive for the subsequent development of Judaism. While there is an abundance of Jewish literature dating from the sixth century BCE onward (e.g., the later books of the Old Testament, and the literature of the Apocrypha and the Dead Sea sect), Iranian literature corresponding to the same period is sadly deficient. Some have therefore argued that Jewish-Persian contact during the sixth to fourth centuries BCE should not be postulated as the contributing factor in the development of parallel ideas in Judaism. Rather, the explanation can be shown to be the development of certain trends inherent in the earlier biblical writings.

While it is not uncommon that similar ideas rise independently under similar (or even different) circumstances, "it does not seem at all likely that so many similarities could have been formed in parallel independently, and, despite the chronological difficulties of the documentation, in most of the parallel points one may feel quite confident that the ideas were indigenous to Iran."[13] Evidence of the similarities between Zoroastrianism and Judaism, Christianity, and Islam are diverse and range from theological to ethical and to eschatological matters. Of particular interest in this respect are the following shared concepts and beliefs:

• God and Satan (or the devil)
• Angels and demons
• Heaven and hell (and Purgatory in Christianity)
• Resurrection of the body and life everlasting
• Individual judgment at death and cosmic last judgment
• Arrival of the Messiah
• Cosmic events during the end of the world
• The Armageddon battle followed by a millennium period

Obviously this is not the place to resolve the argument for or against the influence of Zoroastrianism on the three faiths of Judaism, Christianity, and Islam. Nevertheless, it is hardly conceivable that some of the characteristic ideas and practices in Judaism, Christianity, and Islam came into being without Zoroastrian influence.

CHAPTER FIVE

Zoroastrian Observances

Zoroastrianism, to some modern proponents of the faith, is a matter of individual conviction and reasoned belief. To the majority, however, Zoroastrianism is a body of fixed traditional practices, which are not to be criticized or neglected but observed as a matter of course. For such people, Zoroastrianism is not expressed in doctrinal principles or systems of belief, but observed in prescribed rites and fixed forms of religious behaviour, which shape their lives and endow them with meaning and purpose.

BIRTH

On the occasion of the completion of the fifth and seventh months of pregnancy, most Zoroastrian households light a lamp of clarified butter. Upon the birth of a child a lamp is lit again and kept burning for at least three days in the room where the mother of the child is confined. Some, however, keep the lamp burning for ten days while others maintain it for forty. One explanation for this custom is that the flame wards off evil influences or forces that may inflict damage or harm. Nowadays these practices have fallen into disuse.

The period of confinement of a woman after giving birth is generally forty days (which allows her to be freed from all impurities and defilements) at the end of which she takes a purificatory bath in order to mix and socialize with others. During this state of confinement, food is offered to her on a separate plate, and all persons coming in contact with her, even medical attendants, are to undertake special ablutions. The bedding and clothing used by her are to be destroyed. Nowadays these restrictions and injunctions are not fully observed by all.

The first birthday of a child also marks an important occasion. On that day the child is taken to the fire-temple where, in a religious ceremony, blessings are invoked and spent ashes from the holy fire are applied to the child's forehead.

INITIATION

Between the ages of seven and eleven (in India) and twelve and fifteen (in Iran) a special ceremony known as *Naojote* (or *Navjote*) takes place. *Naojote* is an initiation ceremony that makes a child responsible for honouring Zoroastrian religious observances. The ceremony, which usually, though not necessarily, takes place in the home, consists essentially in investing the child with a sacred shirt (*sudra*, *sudreh*, *sedra*) and a sacred thread or cord (*kusti*, *kustig*). The shirt is a white undershirt (symbol of purity) that has a small pouch at the chest (symbol for storing good deeds). The cord consists of six interwoven strands, each of which is made of twelve white, woollen threads, making a total of seventy-two threads (symbolizing the seventy-two chapters of the Yasna). The six strands are braided together at each end of the cord to form three tassels, each of which contains twenty-four threads. The cord is worn like a belt (or girdle) over the shirt and is to be untied and retied daily on the following occasions: immediately after rising in the morning, at times of bathing, after each call of nature, before reciting prayers, and before eating meals.

Prior to the ceremony, the child is made to undergo a purificatory ritual bath and then taken to a room where parents, relatives, friends, and various priests are assembled. There, the child sits facing eastward (the direction of the rising sun, symbol of Ahura Mazda) on a low stool in front of one of the officiating priests, all of whom are seated on a carpet on the floor. Beside the officiating priest are arrayed the following articles: a tray of rice; a tray of flowers; a lighted lamp and/or burning candle; a tray containing a mixture of pomegranate, rice, grains, raisins, almonds, and a few slices of coconut; a fire in a container; and a tray bearing a new set of clothes for the child, including a sacred shirt and a sacred cord.

The ceremony includes the recitation of various prayers, the confession and declaration of the Articles of Faith (*Fravarane*), the child's investiture with the sacred shirt and cord, and his dressing with the new set of clothes. The declaration of faith is in some ways equivalent to the Christian creed. The initiate affirms belief in Ahura Mazda; praises the value of the moral triad of good thoughts, words, and deeds; proclaims the Mazdayasnian religion to be "the good religion," indeed, the best of all religions past and present, and the source of peace; and confirms that Ahura Mazda is the source of all good things. Here are the words of the declaration of faith:

I profess myself a Mazdean, a follower of Zarathushtra, opposing the demons, accepting the doctrine of Ahura, one who praises the beneficent immortals, who worships the beneficent immortals. I accredit all good things, those that are indeed the best, to Ahura Mazda the good....[1]

The officiating priest next invokes the blessing of Ahura Mazda and then showers various items from the trays over the child's head. The entire ceremony ends with a festive banquet in honour of the Zoroastrian initiate.

Incidentally, in the order of service for the ritual of christening (or baptism), the Armenian church has retained a significant Zoroastrian symbol. After the blessing of the sacred cord (ARM *narod*) and prior to the ceremonial bath comes the recitation of what is commonly known as the renouncement of evil. Holding the neophyte in his arms, the officiating priest recites the following prayer:

Receive, O Lord, who lovest mankind, this child who is being presented to Thee. Cleanse his mind and his thoughts from all the influences of the Adversary and make him worthy to be washed of our old sins ... Keep away and banish, by calling upon him Thy name which conquers all, the thoughts, the words and the deeds of the Evil One, who is accustomed to deceive men and make them perish.[2]

Then the priest places the neophyte in the arms of the godfather, and a very significant symbolic feature follows. The officiating priest, the godfather with the neophyte in his arms, and every present participant turns physically to face west, which represents the realm of the Evil One, and in unison recite the following three times:

We renounce Satan and his every deceit, his wiles, his thoughts, his acts, his evil will, his evil angels, his evil ministers, his evil agents, and his evil will power, renouncing we renounce.[3]

Next, every one turns physically to face east, which represents the realm of the good God, and in unison they recite the following:

We turn to the light of the knowledge of God ...[4]

Thus, the fundamental Zoroastrian feature of human choice in the areas of thought, word, and deed, and the symbolic gestures of facing first westward to the Adversary and then eastward to God, is a marked characteristic in the ritual of christening in Armenian Christianity.

MARRIAGE

The Zoroastrian institution of marriage offers yet another occasion for celebration of an important religious ceremony. On the day of the wedding, before the ceremony, the bride and bridegroom take a sacred bath. The ceremony itself is generally performed in the evening, just a little after sunset, in order to illustrate that just as day and night and light and darkness are united at twilight, so do the bride and groom unite to share prosperity and adversity, happiness and grief.

An hour or two before the celebration of the marriage, a group representing the bride's side of the family forms a procession and proceeds to the bridegroom's home carrying various valuable presents. After presenting them, this group returns home. Next, a procession (sometimes preceded by musicians) composed of the officiating priests, the bridegroom, and members of his group parades to the bride's home. Everyone enters the bride's house except the bridegroom, who stands at the threshold and submits to several welcoming ceremonies: his forehead is marked in red; rice is sprinkled over his head; an egg, a coconut, and a small dish of water are, in turn, passed around his head and then dashed to the ground. The bridegroom then enters, takes his seat, and, after a decent interval, is joined by his bride. The couple sit opposite each other separated by a piece of cloth hung between them as a curtain. A candle burns on each side of the couple and nearby a fire burns in a container. The officiating priests now perform the ceremony of union, which includes symbolic rituals, the exchange of vows, prayers, admonitions, and benedictions. All the assembled guests are then entertained at a marriage feast.

DEATH

Religious observances associated with death and the disposal of the corpse are among the most difficult for Zoroastrians to implement outside their homeland. Zoroastrians who do not live in India or Iran are forced to conform to local conditions, and usually choose the crematorium rather than the cemetery. Wherever possible, however, they observe the following sequence of solemn ritual.

First, the corpse is thoroughly washed and dressed in a clean set of clothes. Next, the sacred cord of the deceased is tied around the corpse, which is placed on a cot while two attendants recite a prayer sitting close by. Two official corpse-bearers now arrive at the home of the deceased to cover the corpse with cloth, remove it from the cot, and place it on slabs of stone in a corner of the front room. Then three circular boundary lines are drawn around the corpse as a safeguard against the spread of impurity.

What follows next is known as the dog-sight (sagdid) ceremony. A dog, generally a "four-eyed" dog (a dog with two eye-like spots just above the eyes), is presented so that it gazes at the corpse. Although various reasons are assigned to this ceremony, the purpose in ancient times was to ascertain whether or not life was altogether extinct. This presentation is repeated several times. After the first gaze, however, fire is brought into the room in an urn. Usually a priest sits before the fire, reciting various prayers and tending it continually with sandalwood and frankincense.

About an hour or so before the removal of the body, two (or four if the body is heavy) corpse-bearers, swathed in white vestments except for their faces, enter the house, place an iron bier by the side of the corpse, recite in a hushed voice the declaration to undertake the ceremony of disposal of the dead (the Dasturi), and then sit silently by the side of the corpse. The recital of this declaration by the corpse-bearers is necessary in order to obtain permission from Ahura Mazda, other divine beings, and past and present important priests to perform the task. This recitation is as follows:

[We do this] with the religious authority of the creator Ahura Mazda, with the religious authority of the beneficent immortals, with the religious authority of righteous Sraosa, with the religious authority of Zarathushtra the Spitamid, with the religious authority of Adurbad, son of Maraspand, [and] with the religious authority of the high priest....[5]

Two priests now stand at a distance from the body and recite the Ahuna Vairya prayer. Half-way through their recitation, they pause for a minute, which signals the corpse-bearers to remove the body from the slabs of stone and place it over the iron bier. When the priests finish the remainder of their recitation, the sagdid is repeated once again, upon which everyone assembled in the house pays their last respects to the deceased.

The corpse-bearers then secure the body to the bier with straps of cloth and carry it from the house to the "Tower of Silence," or funerary tower (*dakhma*), which is a massive, round, tower-like building, generally raised on elevated ground or a hill, where dead bodies are exposed to the sun and to flesh-eating birds. A final *sagdid* follows at the entrance to the tower, after which the body is carried in, stripped of its clothing, and exposed to the sun and the vultures. The bones of the denuded skeleton are left for a while to be dried by the sun and then thrown into a deep well with a deposit of lime and phosphorus.

Zoroastrian communities formed by migration to the West have, quite understandably, abandoned a number of these traditional funeral practices in order to conform to local conventions. Zoroastrians depend on physicians to complete a medical certificate of death and on morticians to make the necessary arrangements for the disposal of the corpse, though some Zoroastrian rites are occasionally performed in funeral homes upon request. Iranian Zoroastrians, except those living in remote villages, have also nowadays abandoned the practice of the tower.

PRAYER

The recitation of prayers plays a major part in all Zoroastrian rites. Three prayers are used most frequently because they are regarded as the holiest and most sacred in the whole of the Avesta. These prayers, known as Ahuna Vairya (or Ahunavar, Ahunwar), Ashem Vohu, and Yenhe Hatam, are variously characterized as sacred formulas, spells, chants, or mantras. No matter what term is used, their importance and sacredness can hardly be exaggerated. They are presumed to be so potent and efficacious that they form a part of virtually every Zoroastrian litany. In fact, the recitation of these ancient Gathic, brief, and efficacious prayers is considered the highest service rendered to Ahura Mazda, and a substitute for offering any other prayers to him. The following translation represents one of several renderings:[6]

Ahuna Vairya
As [is] the lord, so should the judge be chosen in accordance with the righteousness. Establish the power of actions that result from a life with good purpose for Mazda and the lord who was made shepherd for the poor.

Ashem Vohu
Righteousness [is] good, it is best. According to [our] wish it is, according to our wish it shall be. Righteousness belongs to Asa Vahista.

Yenhe Hatam
We worship all those male and female beings whom Ahura Mazda knows are best for worship according to righteousness.

These brief, important prayers are memorized by Zoroastrians and transmitted by word of mouth from generation to generation.

PRIESTHOOD

Zoroastrian priesthood is a hereditary office. Only the sons of a Zoroastrian priest or the male descendants of a priestly family are considered for priestly office. There are several ceremonies to be fulfilled before a man may perform any priestly function. On completion of the *navar* ceremony, the candidate becomes an *ervad* and can perform ordinary services. After undergoing the *martab* ceremony he becomes a *mobed*, and is fully qualified to perform all ceremonies. A *dastur* is the authorized head of any group of priests belonging to a particular congregation or a particular fire-temple.

PURITY-IMPURITY

The Zoroastrian concept of a universal conflict between the forces of good and evil is best exemplified in the ritual linked with the paired concepts of purity and impurity, symbolizing good and evil respectively.[7] In other words, ritual practices and symbolic gestures sustain the Zoroastrian doctrine of cosmic dualism, and there is no better evidence for this than the purificatory observances. They provide the best means whereby each Zoroastrian becomes the central protagonist in the cosmic battle between the forces of good and evil in the material world. Any violation of purity rites is considered an act of impurity, which furthers the cause of evil. This means that Zoroastrian acts of purification serve as a means to ensure, both on a personal and communal level, the triumph of good over evil. However, in no way do these acts provide an expiation from sin – a notion central to Judaism, Christianity, and Islam.

Zoroastrian purificatory rituals are usually grouped into three categories. The most important category is the *Bareshnum* (or *Barashnum i no shab*), which ought to be undertaken by every devotee at least once in a lifetime. The next category comprises three rituals observed on special occasions: *Padyab, Nahn,* and *Riman.* The final category includes various acts to ensure a continuous state of personal and communal virtue and purity.

Bareshnum

The *Bareshnum* is considered the highest form of purification and is restricted almost always nowadays either to candidates for the priesthood or to priests who desire to qualify themselves for the performance of certain religious ceremonies (Videvdat 8, 9, 19; Persian Rivayats 593, 595–596). Iranian Zoroastrians occasionally perform the ritual on children and adults who either suffer from impurities of birth or have been polluted through contact with carrion.[8] The Ilm i Khshnum (an Indian Zoroastrian occult movement) permit laypersons as well as priests to undergo this purification ritual.[9]

The *Bareshnum* ritual consists of three ceremonial baths performed with the aid of two priests over a nine-night (ten-day) period of retreat. A preliminary bath at the fire-temple is followed by various purificatory rituals: a total of eighteen applications of each of *nirangdin* (consecrated bull's urine), sand, and water; the presentation of a dog thirteen times; and the recitation of various prayers. The candidate, however, observes various specified practices, including meditation and prayer, during the entire period.

The function of the *Bareshnum* is to regain and maintain ritual purity. The site chosen to conduct this ceremony was originally an open, desolate area. Today, the ritual is performed within circular (in Iran) or rectangular (in India) compounds to secure religious sanctity and privacy from the majority non-Zoroastrian population. The performance of the ritual itself is considered highly efficacious in aiding the soul's journey ultimately to heaven. The efficacy of the ritual, however, may be vitiated if, for instance, there is any impurity either within the confined compounds or in the purificatory liquids, if it rains during the performance of the ritual, if nocturnal emission of semen occurs during the period of retreat, or if the candidate dies in the compound.

Most priests try to maintain their state of purity for as long as possible after undergoing the *Bareshnum* ritual. Consequently, they follow rigorously rules necessary to ensure ritual purity. For instance, they avoid contact with menstruating women, bathhouse attendants, barbers, corpse-bearers, and non-Zoroastrians. They cut their own hair, refuse to eat food prepared by non-Zoroastrians, and are very careful not to swallow a tooth, or bleed, or be burned. The violation of any of these rules vitiates the efficacy of the ritual, necessitating a repeat of the *Bareshnum* ceremony. Iranian Zoroastrians have developed a unique practice, unparalleled among Indian Zoroastrians. They can formally confer ritual purity to a sweet pomegranate tree by tying seven knots with a green or white thread to its trunk while reciting the Ahuna Vairya (or Ahunawar) prayer.[10]

Padyab

All three of the secondary rituals, the *Padyab*, *Nahn*, and *Riman*, are less rigorous than the *Bareshnum* and are therefore undertaken more frequently by most Zoroastrians. These rituals are performed regularly at set times, or on specific occasions during one's life. Their observance ensures and maintains personal and communal purity of body, mind, and soul.

The *Padyab* is a simple form of ablution that is performed several times a day: in the morning after rising; after answering calls of nature; before taking meals; and before saying prayers. This rite consists of three parts: the recitation of a short prayer formula; the washing of the face and exposed parts of the body, such as the hands or feet; and the untying and retying of the sacred cord with the recital of a special formula.

Nahn

The *Nahn* is a sacred bath of purification that requires the services of a priest and is conducted either at the candidate's home or within the premises of a fire-temple. The ritual is performed only during daylight hours (since darkness belongs to evil) and is observed on the following special occasions: the *Naojote* (initiation) ceremony; the marriage ceremony; forty days after childbirth; and on any one day during the ten-day *Farvardegan* (or *Frawardigan*) holiday, which marks the end of the Zoroastrian year.

The ceremony associated with this form of purification consists of the following: the observance of *Padyab*; the chewing of a pomegranate leaf (symbolic of fecundity, fertility, and everlasting life); the drinking of a few drops of consecrated bull's urine (*nirang*); the recital of the Repentance Prayer; the application of unconsecrated bull's urine (*gomez*) over the body from the head downwards; the performance of a sacred bath; and dressing in a set of new clothes, including a prayer cap.

A more complex purification ritual, called the *Si-Shuy Nahn*, is administered to those who have come in contact with impure materials, particularly carrion or bodily refuse (Persian Rivayats 88.2.2–6). Usually, this ablution ritual is performed at a desolate site (as in India) rather than at home (as in Iran), and the priest maintains his distance from the candidate to prevent the spreading of impurity to either himself or the community. In addition to administering the regular *Nahn* rites mentioned above, the candidate is required to undergo the application of unconsecrated bull's urine (*gomez*), dust (fire ash), and water nine times, followed by a final threefold application of water. Each successive performance of ablution diminishes the individual's impurity until full purity is regained.

Riman

The third form of purification, called *Riman*, requires the services of two attendants (one of whom must be a priest) and is presently confined strictly to those who have come in contact with corpses in the course of ministering to the dead. Like all other purificatory rites, the *Riman* is administered only during daylight hours and only at sites isolated from the general public – that is, never within the confines of a fire-temple or a home. The materials for the purificatory ceremony consist of consecrated and unconsecrated bull's urine, dust (fire ash), water, pomegranate leaves, two shallow metallic bowls, two empty eggshells, a metal container, a high-necked vessel, and a stick made of twigs. All of these must be discarded at the end of the ceremony to prevent the spread of impurity.

The candidate who seeks purification stands naked at a distance from the attendants. If the candidate is a female, the priest stands behind a partition and instructs the female assistant to conduct the actual administration of the ritual. The candidate then chews the pomegranate leaves; drinks the consecrated bull's urine from the eggshell in three sips; breaks and tosses the eggshell into a pit; applies to his body fifteen times in sequence the unconsecrated bull's urine, dust, and water contained in the second eggshell and the metallic bowls, extended to him by means of the stick made of twigs; washes the body with water poured from the vessel by one of the attendants; dries with a clean towel; dresses in a new set of clothes; and ties the sacred cord.

When the ceremony ends, the priest then discards all the purificatory materials by placing them into a pit, which is then filled with earth and sealed. Now the priest and his assistant return to the fire-temple and ritually rid themselves of all traces of impurities by applying unconsecrated urine and water.

In recent years, there has been a decline in the practice of this form of purification, particularly among Indian Zoroastrians. For whatever reason, corpse-bearers now perform a simple ablution with unconsecrated bull's urine after each funeral, and their families are no longer regarded as impure.

Daily Rites

All daily life is governed by rules that reflect the Zoroastrian doctrine of dualism. Certain bodily substances – such as hair, nails, skin, breath, saliva, blood, urine, feces, semen, and menstrual fluid – are all considered to be impure once they leave or are separated from the body. Any contact with such substances (known as *hikhra*, *hixra*, meaning excrement) renders a Zoroastrian ritually impure and therefore necessitates certain purificatory acts. Elaborate codes also exist to prevent food, utensils, clothing, and homes from contamination by these substances.

Thus, there are specific rituals to be performed for cutting hair and paring nails. Indeed, a proper fulfilment of the ritual requires a specified disposal rite. Although variant forms of practices among Iranian and Indian Zoroastrians have continued into modern times, at present only priests and a few orthodox Zoroastrians still follow these rituals. Most Zoroastrians now visit a professional barber or hairdresser, and pare their nails without any precautionary or purificatory acts.

Precautions taken to prevent the state and spread of impurity to the seven creations of Ahura Mazda (vegetation, animals, earth, water, metal, fire, and human beings) by breath and saliva are still carefully observed. Naturally, these precautions are difficult to observe during everyday activities, but the release of breath and saliva must be controlled as much as possible so that it does not come in contact with any sacred elements or substances. This practice is strictly enforced during religious rituals. Every priest engaged in a religious rite wears a white veil covering mouth and nose so as not to transmit any impurities released by his breath or spittle.

In mundane matters, Zoroastrians are enjoined to control as much as possible sneezing, sighing, and yawning, because all of these activities release breath and saliva into the surrounding area. Similarly, Zoroastrians are asked to refrain from drinking from a glass or cup used by another person before washing it properly with water. Taking food from a common dish is also proscribed since impurities could be transmitted by traces of saliva on the fingertips. Also to be avoided are blowing the nose in public, and spitting water, food, or saliva onto the ground. Nowadays, most of these precautionary acts of purification have fallen into disuse by all except a few orthodox individuals.

The elaborate precautionary rituals associated with urination and excretion, and the rigid enforcement of rules governing sex, semen, nocturnal emission, menstrual flow, miscarriage, and stillbirth, have all been abandoned by the majority of Zoroastrians, who consider such ritual ablutions totally outmoded by modern ideological standards. Similarly, all dietary restrictions that once regulated the Zoroastrian daily consumption of food have been either relaxed or totally discarded by both Iranian and Indian Zoroastrians. Previously, all living creatures were divided into three groups: the good (*ahuric*), the evil (*daevic*), and the neutral (those creatures neutralized by Ahura Mazda for everyone's benefit). Today, the flesh and products of all kinds of creatures are freely consumed according to one's taste and desire. However, any food that has come in contact with carrion or the substances called "excrement" (*hikhra*) is still considered impure and therefore promptly discarded.

Thus, all Zoroastrian purificatory acts, including the consecration and use of sacred elements and utensils, are ultimately directed to combat cosmic evil. This symbolic value has played a significant role in the survival of the Zoroastrian faith throughout the centuries. But it is also equally important to realize that purity practices, even in their simplified versions, have served, and continue to serve, as a means of expressing symbolically the essential Zoroastrian eschatological beliefs. Every Zoroastrian devotee yearns for the final salvation of the universe and the immortality of human beings. By performing these purificatory rituals, every devotee is reminded that evil, pain, suffering, and death can be counteracted and transcended until the final day of victory, when perfection and immortality shall reign forever.

YASNA

The Yasna (or Yazishan, meaning "sacrifice", "dedication") is the most important ritual in the Zoroastrian tradition; performed daily during the morning watch, it takes about two and a half hours.[11] The Yasna serves two purposes: to offer sacrifice (or worship) to Ahura Mazda, the Amesha Spenta, the Yazata, and all the spiritual forces; and to invest the priests with the necessary ritual powers (Dadestan i Dinig 48; Denkard 8.46). Tradition has it that, just as Ahura Mazda created the material world by the performance of Yasna, so also his triumph will be inaugurated when he performs the final Yasna at the end of time.

The Yasna is performed by two priests – a chief officiating priest (*zot*) and an assistant priest (*raspi*) – in a special consecrated and demarcated area (known as *pawi*) within the precinct of the fire-temple. The demarcated area is divided into a number of rectangular spaces, each of which contains its required liturgical objects. The size of the demarcated area varies according to the available space, but the placement of the liturgical objects within the demarcated area follows a structured pattern.

On the south side of the demarcated area stands a fire-table, made of a flat slab of stone with legs of stone, upon which a fire-urn (*afringanyu*) is placed. The fire-urn contains a fine grey ash that helps maintain the fire placed on it during the preparatory ceremony called *paragna* (or *paragra*). Beside the fire-table and slightly to the west are two blocks of stone on which sandalwood and frankincense are placed, to be used as an offering at the end of the preparatory ceremony, and again at certain points during the Yasna ritual. A large tray is also placed next to the fire-table containing a pair of tongs for picking up wood-chips or embers, a ladle for placing the sandalwood and frankincense in the fire, and large pieces of sandalwood for feeding into the fire whenever necessary. To the right of this tray is a long-necked metal vessel, which is placed on a metal stand at the left side of the tray after its use in the ritual.

Moving northward, close to the centre of the demarcated area is the ritual table, made also of a flat stone slab with legs of stone, upon which various sacred implements, including a bundle of twenty-one metallic wires (*barsom*), are placed. Next to the ritual table toward the west is a small metal container located on a stone block for pouring water. Beside this container and slightly to the north is a larger water container placed on a large stone base. Two small cups for refilling water, and a pestle and a shallow bowl pierced with holes for pounding and filtering *hom* (the *haoma* plant), are kept in this container until their use in the preparatory ceremony.

On the north side of the demarcated area and immediately in front of the ritual table is a square stool, made of a slab of stone and covered with a piece of cloth or mat, on which the assistant priest sits during the preparatory ceremony, and later the officiating priest during the Yasna ritual. Behind this stone stool and outside of the demarcated area are two more containers, one for fetching milk and the other for storing consecrated *hom* juice.

Priests who perform the Yasna ritual undergo purificatory rites, recite special prayers, dress in a prescribed attire, and cover their noses and mouths with a white veil. The purpose of the veil, as stated above, is to protect the consecrated ceremonial elements and implements from contamination by the breath and spittle of the priests. The lines of demarcation surrounding the ceremony area are an additional protection against all impurities. Consequently, no unauthorized or unqualified person is allowed to cross the boundary lines of the sacred precinct during the performance of the ceremony. The ceremony is considered invalid if anyone breaks the rule.

Preceding the Yasna ritual is a preliminary ceremony called *paragna*, in which all the implements and elements of the Yasna ritual are consecrated and safeguarded from impurities by the assistant priest.[12] The material elements consecrated in this preparatory ceremony are: water, butter, bread, milk, twigs or pomegranate, a date-palm leaf, *hom*, sandalwood, and frankincense. The application of ash and water, mantric utterances, and several elaborate ritual actions accompanied by recitation from the Avesta bestow on all the implements and elements the highest degree of purity.

The ceremonial acts of the *paragna* establish a close connection between the spiritual (*menog*) and material (*getig*) realms. Indeed, the notion of ritual purity is intimately bound up with the ideas of righteousness and goodness. By consecrating and presenting tangible offerings to Ahura Mazda, the Amesha Spenta, and the Yazata, the priest is inviting their presence; it is believed that they derive their strength and pleasure from such sacrifices. Furthermore, the presence and use of specific kinds of material elements commands the attention of the heptad (Ahura Mazda plus the six Amesha Spenta) associated with them. In return, the priest, his fellow worshippers, and the entire good creation of Ahura Mazda all receive from the spiritual realm equally tangible blessings in the form of increase, prosperity, and ultimately universal renovation and salvation.

Thus, the ritual power of a priest is derived from ceremonial or liturgical actions, including the recitation of holy scriptures. The utterances of Avestan words carry an inherent power that makes them doubly effective. Such text recitations dislodge Ahriman and his associates and prevent them from causing harm to humanity and the created world of Ahura Mazda.

The fundamental purpose, then, of the *paragna* is to establish purity so that the Yasna ritual that follows it (and others like the Videvdat and Visparad rituals) will effectively bring pleasure, benefit, and blessings to all the divine beings, as well as to all the good creation of Ahura Mazda, including the faithful followers of "the good religion". The material world, according to Zoroastrian doctrine, is not evil. It is the arena in which humans join the spiritual forces to combat evil. Thus, the performance of the Yasna ritual is considered to be a key weapon in the struggle against evil. So vital is the performance of the Yasna ritual that without it the world would ultimately end in total destruction at the hands of Ahriman and his associates. At the end of time, when Ahura Mazda will perform the final Yasna ritual, this material world will be completely purified, renovated, and transformed.

The performance of the Yasna ritual is primarily a priestly function, requiring no audience. Nonetheless, a number of devotees attend the ritual and remain throughout the entire performance. During the Yasna ceremony, Ahura Mazda and all his invisible, spiritual powers are reverently invoked through special formulas and through the ceremonial recitation and dedication of the seventy-two chapters of the Yasna, including the seventeen chapters containing the Gathas of Zoroaster. The priest consumes the consecrated elements of bread and milk. At the conclusion of the ceremony, a portion of the consecrated *hom* is poured into a well as a symbolic gesture of offering to the benevolent spirit of the water. The remainder of the libation, along with the bread, is consumed by attending worshippers. This last act is known as *chashni*, signifying the act of communion with the forces of the spiritual world. The Yasna ritual is officially concluded when the priests offer a prayer of thanks to the holy fire (Yasna 62).

VIDEVDAT

Another liturgical service, also conducted in the sacred precinct of the Zoroastrian fire-temple by qualified priests, is the Videvdat ceremony, which is usually performed sometime between midnight and dawn. The recitation from the Yasna texts and the objects dedicated to Ahura Mazda in the Yasna ritual are used here too, but with an additional difference. The ceremony includes the recitation of the Visparad and the reading of the Videvdat to invoke the spiritual beings and ward off the demons, and offerings are dedicated at the conclusion of the service to coincide with sunrise.

FIRE

No Zoroastrian ritual or religious ceremony is complete without the presence of the holy fire.[13] The flame is considered to be the visible sign of Ahura Mazda's presence, the symbol of his truth (*asha*). According to tradition, fire was used by Ahura Mazda in the creation of cattle and human beings (Bundahishn 1.3), and fire will be used again by him when he brings about the final renovation of the universe (Zadspram 34.50). Thus, fire is highly venerated and used as an object of worship among Zoroastrians.[14]

The fire of the highest grade (known as *Atash Bahram* or *Atash Varahran*) has the power to attract all the divine beings. It is kept in principal temples and is enthroned as a king with a crown above it (Videvdat 8.81). All sacred fires, whether for temple or domestic use, should be kept constantly burning. To extinguish the fire is believed to be a grave sin. Furthermore, fire (like water) is considered to be extremely vulnerable to pollution. Consequently, placing or dropping objects into it, other than those that are considered ritually pure, is believed to contribute to impurity. Only pieces of clean, dry, fragrant wood (such as sandalwood, aloe, benzoin) and frankincense should be offered to a fire. For this reason, Zoroastrians have often been categorized as either "fire-worshippers" or "sun-worshippers." They themselves vehemently repudiate such misnomers. Fire, represented especially by the sun, is regarded as a symbol of divine purity, light, power, and warmth. While it is a very important symbol in their worship, it is not worshipped as a deity.

Interestingly, Herodotus (3.16) noticed this veneration of fire and wrote: "Persians hold fire to be a god, and never burn their dead." Indeed, because fire is susceptible to impurity, Zoroastrians have developed several strict rules to prevent the defilement of a fire. For instance, the faithful are instructed to leave all cooking pots one-third empty to prevent their contents from boiling over and polluting the flames (Persian Rivayats 66.1.1–67). No waste or garbage is to be burned in a fire. The presence of fire should always be kept three paces away from impure substances (*hikhra*), fifteen paces from the sight of menstruating women, and thirty paces from corpses or carrion. And a small fire should be kept burning in a home where a person or a dog has died, to ward off the demons of death that are lurking round about.

Devout Zoroastrians attend fire-temples daily. The less observant attend at least on four sacred days each month. Before entering the fire-temple, shoes are removed, hands and feet washed (the feet are washed only if they have been exposed by not wearing socks, stockings, or shoes on the way to the temple), and a prayer is recited praising Ahura Mazda and condemning Ahriman. Next, the worshipper enters the temple, where the sacred fire is burning, and receives ashes from the priest. After reciting a prayer, the worshipper retires backwards, always facing the sacred fire.

The presence and veneration of fire in all Zoroastrian rituals is considered to be a symbolic action in the struggle against spiritual demons, death, and impurity. This symbolic association is attested to in the Avesta, where fire is described as the "divine purifier" who "takes away impurity" and "grants health and prosperity" (Yasna 25.7, 36.1; Ataxsh Niyayishn 1.1). Similarly, the glory believed to reside in the enthroned fires within the Zoroastrian fire-temples is thought to wage war against all spiritual demons and material impurities (Zadspram 3.82–83).

MEMORIAL AND FESTIVALS

Zoroastrians observe a number of special days and religious festivals. To list these special days according to the Gregorian calendar is misleading, since the Zoroastrian calendar is solar and consists of twelve months of thirty days each. Five additional days, called *gatha*, bring the total days in a year to 365. The following are the names of the twelve months in the Zoroastrian calendar:

1	Farvardin	7	Meher (Mihr)
2	Ardibehesht	8	Avan (Aban)
3	Khordad	9	Adar (Azar)
4	Tir	10	Dey
5	Amardad	11	Bahman
6	Shahrevar	12	Aspandarmad (Sipandarmaz)

The week has no place in the Zoroastrian calendar; a month of thirty days is the only sub-unit. The names of the days are as follows:

1	Hormazd	16	Meher
2	Bahman	17	Sarosh
3	Ardibehesht	18	Rashn
4	Shahrevar	19	Farvardin
5	Aspandarmad	20	Bahram
6	Khordad	21	Ram
7	Amardad	22	Govad
8	Daepadar	23	Daepdin
9	Adar	24	Din
10	Avan	25	Ashishvangh
11	Khorshed	26	Ashtad
12	Mohor	27	Asman
13	Tir	28	Zamyad
14	Gosh	29	Mahraspand
15	Daepmeher	30	Aneran

The five additional (*gatha*) days are:

1 Ahunavad   4 Vahukhshathra
2 Ushtavad   5 Vahishtoisht
3 Spentomad

Each day of the month is presided over by an Amesha Spenta or Yazata, except that four days of each month are sacred to Ahura Mazda.

Many Zoroastrians observe a number of festivals scrupulously. Some of these festivals are seasonal feasts, such as the *gahambars*, that last five days. The fifth day is usually considered the most solemn day and is observed with liturgical services and the communal eating of offerings. Other important historical events and religious anniversaries are generally celebrated with *jashan* (praise)services.

The dates of some of the more important observances in the Zoroastrian calendar have long been in dispute and, some two hundred years ago, caused a permanent division among Zoroastrians. At present there are three different factions. One group, known as the Kadimi (meaning "Ancient"), favour the old calendar; a second group, the Shenshahi (or Shahenshah, meaning "Imperial"), use a calendar one month behind that of the Kadimi; while a third group, the Fasli (meaning "Seasonal"), base their calculations on the present national calendar of Iran. The following are some of the more important occasions.

New Year's Day (*Nao Roz*) is one of the most important dates in the Zoroastrian calendar. The Kadimi observe the New Year in August, the Shenshahi observe it in September, while the Fasli celebrate the New Year on 21 March. All three groups, however, celebrate the festival with great feasting and ceremony.

The ten days preceding New Year's Day are sacred and reserved for the remembrance of dead relatives. A special place is set aside either at home or in the fire-temple. Silver vases dedicated on this occasion to dead relatives are placed on a marble table and kept filled with fresh flowers. A lamp is kept burning, as well as the sacred fire. Prayers and ceremonies are offered daily in remembrance of the dead. The last five days are particularly solemn days and belong to the *Hamas-path-maedem-ghambar*, also known as the Gatha days. On these days, devout Zoroastrians recite the Gathas of Zoroaster.

Zoroastrians also celebrate the birthday of their prophet Zoroaster (Khordad Sal) on the sixth day of the month of Farvardin (26 March). The occasion is marked with great solemnity and prayers. Feasts (*jashan* and *gahambar*) conclude the celebration. The ceremony commemorating the death of Zoroaster (*Zarthost-no-diso*) is also celebrated with great veneration, and worshippers attend the fire-temple, reciting prayers in honour of their prophet.

Like the Christian festival of All Souls' Day, Zoroastrians also observe in September a memorial to their departed ones (*Farvardingan*). Sandalwood is offered in the temples and flowers are left at the Tower of Silence (*Dakhma*), since there are no cemeteries.

MODERN TRENDS

The pervasive western influence, which seems unquestionably to gain momentum on a global scale, is affecting Zoroastrians all over the world.[15] The Zoroastrian religion, like most others, is unable to ignore the powerful force of western technology, atomic energy, electronic revolution, and space travel. Ancient value systems are being questioned and traditional patterns are being threatened. Will this apparently divisive force prove to be a benefit to all those who today follow the Zoroastrian faith?

Among Zoroastrians, the effect of western ideas is to encourage reform. Attempts are made to curb excessive ceremonialism. Time-honoured teachings and customs are subjected to western-style scientific methods of historical criticism. As a result, conservative and reformist forces are in conflict, with neither side winning a clear victory. A few instances will suffice to indicate this difficulty.

Some Zoroastrian reformists insist that, in spite of the evident cosmic dualism between Ahura Mazda and Ahriman, the basic teaching of Zoroaster, and hence of Zoroastrianism, is monotheistic. Conservative Zoroastrians, however, continue to honour the Yazata and all other divine beings who preside over the various elements and the days of the week, thus embracing a belief that is decidedly polytheistic. Again, heaven and hell, according to reformists, are simply mental constructions, just as Ahriman is one's own creation of evil; conservatives, naturally, resist such rationalistic approaches. Reformists are critical of beliefs that they regard as superstitions and of obscure practices embedded in Zoroastrianism. Criticism of prayers, ceremonials, and teachings has led to widespread scepticism. The use of bull's urine for ritual cleansing, the attendance of a dog to gaze at the corpse during funerary rites, the exposure of corpses on towers, the time-honoured spells and prayers considered efficacious – all these observances once performed in India and Iran are now scoffed at by the reformists. Conservatives, on the other hand, despise any tampering with tradition, reject alternative methods, and cling tenaciously to the ancient religious practices.

Another issue that has provoked considerable debate among conservatives and reformists is that of conversion. The word "convert" (*juddin*) is often used to refer to the admission into the community of a non-Zoroastrian spouse, children of mixed marriages, adopted children, or any individual persuaded by his/her own volition. In other words, the controversy revolves around the question of how far the Zoroastrian community should give up its exclusiveness and accept new believers. This unresolved discussion, which has been going on for more than two centuries, is debated on two levels: the religious-historical and the social-economic. Closely related to the issue of converts is the demographic problem of the community.[16] Declining numbers in the Zoroastrian community suggest possible extinction in the near future. How to redress this catastrophe immediately and effectively has caused irritation and disharmony in the Zoroastrian community.

Many Zoroastrians have entirely abandoned the ancient symbols of their religion: the wearing of the sacred shirt and cord. Others do not feel any strong attachment to their religion, seldom visit the fire-temples, and take little interest in community affairs. To the consternation of the conservatives, certain reformists, influenced by western agnosticism and scepticism, blend their own beliefs with teachings from Hinduism, Christianity, Theosophy, and other religions.

And yet, many Zoroastrians are totally unaffected by the attempts to introduce change. To such individuals, the central structure of the Zoroastrian faith remains the same: to recognize the truth of "the good religion" by strictly adhering to its beliefs and practices. Two ancient sayings reinforce their position:

I shall never apostatize from the Good Religion of the worshipers of Ohrmazd, and I have no doubts concerning it. I neither approve of nor respect other religions, nor do I lend them credence.[17]

I have always been anxious to know God and have been curious in searching out his religion and his will. So I frequented many different sects until, by the grace of God and the power and glory and strength of the Good Religion, I escaped from the abyss of darkness and of doubts that were with difficulty dispelled.[18]

Why do Zoroastrians call their religion "the good religion"? Because they firmly believe that Ahura Mazda is good. Consequently, Zoroastrians attach a special importance to the life-affirming and active dimensions of their faith. Indeed, to actively support the powers of good is, to Zoroastrians, the way to salvation. The ideas of fatalism, of original sin, of resignation or renunciation of earthly happiness, of asceticism, of mysticism, of contemplation, of being absorbed in God or Nirvana, and of rebirth or metempsychosis are all foreign to Zoroastrian teachings. In fact, the opposite is precisely maintained. No other religion expresses as clearly as Zoroastrianism the affirmation of life, the upholding of "the good principle," and the appeal to be active in shaping the world.

Naturally, the world is far from being perfect or complete; it is instead a battlefield for the confrontation between Ahura Mazda and Ahriman. Devout Zoroastrians are urged therefore to join this cosmic fight by their own free will (*vasah*) in order to support "the good principle" and to help the good to its final triumph. Renunciation, asceticism, and all other means that reject life are considered a betrayal of the good powers. Supporting "the good principle" means to fight against vice, lies, immorality, idleness, misfortune, illness, vermin, pests, and all other evil powers that threaten and impair life. Thus, many Zoroastrians make an essential contribution to the victory of the good by knowing and observing "the good religion."

Glossary

ABBREVIATIONS

AR   Arabic
ARM   Armenian
AV   Avestan
GK   Greek
GU   Gujarati
IN   Indian
OP   Old Persian
PER   Persian
PHL   Pahlavi
RV   Rig Veda
SAN   See Sanjana, P.B. in Bibliography
SKT   Sanskrit

Abistag (PHL)   Same as Avesta.

Afringan (PHL)   A common ceremony of blessings, which can be performed in any clean place.

Agiary   Parsee term for a Zoroastrian fire-temple or place of worship.

Ahriman   Adversary; arch-enemy of Ahura Mazda.

Ahuna Vairya (AV)   One of the most efficacious prayers; it begins with the Avestan phrase *yatha ahu vairyo* and has twenty-one words corresponding to the twenty-one books of the Avesta.

Ahunvar (PHL)   Same as Ahuna Vairya.

Ahura Mazda   The Almighty God; Ohrmazd in Pahlavi.

Amahraspandan (PHL)   Same as Amesha Spenta.

Ameretat (AV)   Long life; immortality.

Amesha Spenta (AV)   Immortality; the Holy Immortal presiding over vegetation.

Amurdad (PHL)   Same as Ameretat.

Angra Mainyu   See Ahriman.

Arda Viraf (PER)   The name of a priest of the Sasanian period who saw visions of heaven and hell.

Ardafrawash (PHL)   Spirits of the departed.

Ardag Viraz (PHL)   Same as Arda Viraf.

Ardibehesht (PER)   Same as Asha Vahishta.

Ardvahisht (PHL)   Same as Asha Vahishta.

Asha (AV)   Truth, Order, Righteousness; a principle that governs the world; the first of six divine powers.

Asha Vahishta (AV)   Best Righteousness; the Holy Immortal presiding over fire.

Ashavant   A follower of Asha, or Truth; always contrasted with Dregvant.

Ashem vohu (AV)   One of the holy prayers, which praises righteousness.

Atar   Fire; refers also to the "flaming fire of thought."

Atash (PHL/PER)   A general term for fire.

Atash Bahram (PER)   A consecrated fire of the highest grade.

Avesta (PER)   The name applied to the entire body of sacred books (SCRIPTURES) of the Zoroastrians.

Bahman (PER)   Same as Vohu Manah.

Bandagi (PER)   Prayer.

Barashnom (PHL)   Ritual ablution; part of nine-night (ten-day) purification rite.

Barsom (PHL)   Bundle of twigs held by the officiating priest at acts of worship; nowadays metal wires are substituted for twigs.

Behesht (PER)   Paradise.

Chinvat (PHL)   Bridge over an abyss.

Dadgah   Sacred fire of the third grade.

Daeva (AV)   Demon, evil spirit, evil deity.

Dakhma (AV)   Originally a grave or tomb; later a place of exposure for the dead, the Tower of Silence where a corpse is exposed to birds of prey.

Dastur (PER)   One in authority, a high priest.

Dregvant   A follower of the *druj*.

Druj (AV)   Lie, falsehood, disorder; a principle opposed to *asha*.

Duraosha   Death-dispelling.

Fireshte (PER)   A spirit worthy of worship; a term interchangeable with *yazad*.

Fravashi (AV)   A synonym for the soul; guardian spirit of the soul; a divine essence in human form.

Gah (PHL/PER)   A watch, or period of the day.

Gahambar (PHL/PER)   Six seasonal festivals commemorating the six creations.

Gatha (AV)   Hymns or songs.

Getig (PHL)   Physical, material world, distinguished from *menog*.

Gomez (PHL)   Unconsecrated bull's urine.

Hamestagan (PHL)   The neutral place between heaven and hell.

Haoma (AV)   Sacred plant whose juice is used in Zoroastrian ritual.

Haurvatat (AV)   Health, Perfection; the Holy Immortal presiding over water.

Hordad (PHL)   Same as Haurvatat.

Jashan (PHL/PER)   Act of worship.

Khshathra Vairya (AV)   Desirable, Dominion; the Holy Immortal.

Kusti (PER)   Sacred cord or thread worn from the time of initiation.

Magi   Sing. *magus*, Latin form of Old Persian *magu*, meaning "priest."

Menog (PHL)   Spiritual world, distinguished from *getig*.

Naojote (GU)   A ceremony of investiture, when the sacred shirt and cord are bestowed.

Nask (PHL)   Book, or volume.

Nirang (PHL)   Consecrated bull's urine.

Nirangdin (PHL)   The most exalted and elaborate liturgy, culminating in the consecration of bull's urine.

Niyayesh (PER)   A litany, five in number.

Ohrmazd (PHL)   Same as Ahura Mazda.

Padan (PHL)   A cloth face-mask worn by a priest during rituals.

Patet (PHL)   Prayer of penance.

Raspi (PHL)   Assistant priest.

Sagdid (PHL)   A dog's gaze; seen by a dog.

Shahrevar (PER)   The Holy Immortal presiding over metals; see Khshatriya Vairya.

Spandarmad (PHL)   Same as Spenta Armaiti.

Spenta Armaiti (AV)   Holy Devotion, Bountiful; the Holy Immortal presiding over the earth.

Sudreh (PER)   Sacred shirt worn from the time of initiation.

Vohuman (PHL)   Same as Vohu Mana.

Vohu Mana (AV)   Good Mind; the Holy Immortal presiding over the second day of the Zoroastrian calendar.

Yasht (PHL)   A hymn of praise to an individual divine being.

Yazad (PHL)   Same as *yazata*.

Yazata (AV)   A divine being created or evoked by God and worthy of worship.

Yenghe hatam (AV)   The beginning words of a short, ancient prayer, considered to be extremely efficacious.

Yima   God of death.

Zend   Translation of the Avesta, with commentary in the vernacular language.

Zot   Chief officiating priest.

Notes

1 Burrow, "The Proto-Indoaryans," 123–40; Bosch-Gimpera, "The Migration Route of the Indo-Aryans," 513–17; Young, "The Iranian Migration into the Zagros," 11–34; Belenitsky, *The Ancient Civilization of Central Asia*; Frumkin, *Archaeology in Soviet Central Asia*; V.M. Masson & V.I. Sarianidi, *Central Asia, Turkmenia Before the Achaemenids*; Diakonoff, "Media," 36–148; Ghirshman, *L'Iran et la migration des Indo-Aryens et des Iraniens*.

2 For a survey of the Magi and of the divergent scholarly theories, see Yamauchi, *Persia and the Bible*, 467–91.

3 Insler, *The Gathas of Zarathustra*, 81.

4 Ibid., 99.

5 Ibid., 81.

6 The name Vishtaspa is assumed to be philologically the same as Hystaspes, the name of the father of Darius I. The chief sources for this Hystaspes are the inscriptions of Darius and Herodotus 1.209. For the inscriptions see King, Thompson, and Budge, *The Sculptures and Inscription of Darius*, lxi, 1, 84, 85, 93, 152, 159. The identity of Vishtaspa with Hystaspes was made in the fourth century by the Roman historian Ammianus Marcellinus, *History*, XXIII, vi, 32.

7 For suggested explanations of Zoroaster's name, see Jackson, *Zoroaster, The Prophet of Ancient Iran*, 12–14, 147–9, 226–73.

8 Gottheil, "References to Zoroaster in Syriac and Arabic Literature," 24–51.

9 It is generally held that the first scholar to see the composite nature of the form "Zarathushtra" was Eugène Burnouf, *Commentaire sur le Yaçna*, 12–14.

10 For Greek and Roman writers re date of Zoroaster, see Clemen, *Fontes historiae religionis Persicae*, 42, 48, 74; Fox and Pemberton, *Passages in Greek and Latin Literature*, 45–6, 80, 126; Benveniste, *The Persian Religion According to the Chief Greek Texts*, 15; for the current state of the question see Gnoli, *Zoroaster's Time and Homeland*, 163–5.

11 al-Biruni, *The Chronology of Ancient Nations* (trans. Sachau), 17.

12 Shahbazi, "The 'Traditional Date of Zoroaster' Explained," 25–35, demonstrates how Iranians arrived at the traditional date of seventh to sixth centuries BCE ; see also Kingsley, "The Greek Origin of the Sixth Century Dating of Zoroaster," 245–65; Klima, "The Date of Zoroaster," 556–64.

13 Boyce, *A History of Zoroastrianism*, I, 190. She subsequently changed her position to propose a date between 1700 and 1500 BCE; see her work *Zoroastrians: Their Religious Beliefs and Practices*, 18; Burrow, "The Proto-Indoaryàns," 139; Schaeder, "Zarathustras Botschaft von der rechten Ordnung," 575–602; von Wesendonk, *Das Weltbild der Iranier*, 51; Gnoli, *Zoroaster's Time and Homeland*, 176, 227.

14 Dhalla, *History of Zoroastrianism*, xxxi; Bartholomae, *Zarathustra's Leben und Lehre*, ll; Christensen, *Die Iranier*, 214.

15 Christensen, *Die Iranier*, 214.

16 For instance, Bundahishn 34, translated by West, *Pahlavi Texts*, vol. 5, 149–51; Nyberg, "Questions de cosmogonie et de cosmologie mazdéennes," 1–134; 193–244.

17 Hertel, *Die Zeit Zoroasters*, 21, 47.

18 For a detailed discussion of this issue, see Gnoli, *Zoroaster's Time and Homeland*, 23–57.

19 For a discussion of these matters, see Humbach, "About Gopatsah, His Country, and the Khwarezmian Hypothesis," 327–34.

20 For a detailed discussion, see Gnoli, *Zoroaster's Time and Homeland*, 91–127.

21 Haarbrucher, *Abu-'l-Fath' Muhammad asch-Schahrastani' Religionsparthein und Philosophen-Schulen*, 1: 280.

22 Barbier de Meynard, *Dictionnaire géographique, historique et littéraire de la Perse*, 26, 367.

23 Darmesteter and Mills, *The Zend-Avesta*, 4: LVI.

24 Duchesne-Guillemin, *The Western Response to Zoroaster*, 25.

25 Boyce, "Zoroaster the Priest," 22–38.

26 Yarshater, "Iranian Common Beliefs and World-View," 343–58; Boyce, *A History of Zoroastrianism*, I, 22–46; Schwartz, "The Old Eastern Iranian World View According to the Avesta," 640–63; Frye, *The Heritage of Persia*, 37–47; Mayrhofer, *Die Indo-Arier im alten Vorderasien*; Thieme, "The Aryan gods of the Mitanni Treaties," 301–17; Dumézil, *Les dieux des indo-européens*.

27 Lommel, "Anahita-Sarasvati," 405–13.

28 The identity of the *haoma* plant has been a matter of lively discussion since the work of R.G. Wasson, *Soma: Divine Mushroom of Immortality*, who identified the Indian *soma* (Iranian *haoma*) with the fungus *amanita muscaria*. Wasson's work was critically reviewed by Brough, "Soma and Amanita Muscaria," 331–62. This brought a response from Wasson, *Soma and the Fly-agaric: Mr. Wasson's Rejoinder to Professor Brough*; see also Gershevitch, "An Iranist's View of the Soma Controversy," 45–75; and an earlier work by Godbey, "Incense and Poison Ordeals in the Ancient Orient," 221.

29 The literature on the legend of Yima (IN Yama) is quite extensive. For references to discussions prior to 1930, see Gray, *The Foundations of the Iranian Religions*, 14, n. 1. For more recent references, see Boyce, review of Hartman, in *Bulletin of the School of Oriental and African Studies*, vol. 17 (1955): 174–6; and Duchesne-Guillemin, review of Zaehner, in *Indo-Iranian Journal*, vol. 7 (1963–64): 196–207.

30 The problem of the origin of Ahura Mazda has long been a point of controversy. For different views, see Duchesne-Guillemin, *Zoroastre*, 132; Zaehner, *The Dawn and Twilight of Zoroastrianism*, 64; Frye, *The Heritage of Persia*, 55.

31 For a discussion on Angra Mainyu, the Amesha Spentas, and Ahura Mazda, see Boyce, *A History of Zoroastrianism*, 1: 192–228.

32 Insler, *The Gathas of Zarathustra*, 33.

33 Ibid., 61.

34 Ibid., 35.

35 Ibid., 107.

36 Ibid., 97.

37 In defence of Zoroaster's dualism, see among others: Henning, *Zoroaster, Politician or Witch-Doctor?*, 45–6; Dhalla, *Zoroastrian Theology from the Earliest Times to the Present Day*, 47, 247; Shaked, "Some Notes on Ahriman."

38 In defence of Zoroaster's monotheism, see among others: Fox, "Darkness and Light: The Zoroastrian View," 129–37; Gershevitch, "Zoroaster's Own Contribution," 12–28; Zaehner, *The Dawn and Twilight of Zoroastrianism*, 179; Masani, *Zoroastrianism: The Religion of the Good Life*, 69; Duchesne-Guillemin, *Ohrmazd et Ahriman: l'aventure dualiste dans l'antiquité*, 60; Nyberg, "Questions de cosmogonie," 105.

39 Boyce, *A History of Zoroastrianism*, 1: 192–246; Boyd and Crosby, "Is Zoroastrianism Dualistic or Monotheistic?" 557–88.

40 Oxtoby, "Interpretations of Iranian Dualism," 59–70.

41 The question of the first individual to formulate a monotheistic concept is still unresolved. Scholars differ in their views and propose any one of the following: Akhenaten, Moses, Zoroaster.

42 Nyberg, *Die Religionen des Alten Iran*, proposed that Zoroaster was a sha-
   man who emerged not as a reformer so much as a defender of the
   tradition of his Gathic community. For a witty criticism, see Henning,
   Zoroaster, Politician or Witch-Doctor?. See also the work of
   Widengren, *Stand und Aufgaben der iraniischen Religionsgeschichte*, who
   warns scholars to guard against the tendency to judge Zoroaster
   either as a philosopher of the Greek type or as a modern social
   reformer.

CHAPTER TWO

1 The discussion that follows is condensed from Nigosian, "The Religions
   in Achaemenid Persia," 378–86.
2 For the Avesta, see Geldner, *Avesta: The Sacred Books of the Parsis*, or
   Damesteter and Mills, *The Zend-Avesta*. For the Old Persian inscriptions, see Kent, *Old Persian Grammar, Texts, Lexicon*. For archaeological
   finds, see Schmidt, *Persepolis* 1, 2, 3; and Stronach, *Pasargadae*. For
   classical notices, see Herodotus, *Histories*; Xenophon, *Cyropaedia*; and
   Strabo, *Geography*.
3 The identity of King Vishtaspa has been the subject of endless controversy. For the view that takes for granted the identity of Vishtaspa
   with Hystaspes, the father of Darius I, see Herzfeld, "The Iranian
   Religion at the Time of Darius and Xerxes," 20; for an opposing view
   that regards Vishtaspa as the last ruling prince of the legendary Kavyan
   (Kayanian) dynasty, see Boyce, *A History of Zoroastrianism*, 1: 105.
   Boyce follows Christensen's arguments for the historicity of the
   Kavyans, Christensen, *Les Kayanides*.
4 Benveniste, *The Persian Religion According to the Chief Greek Texts*;
   Duchesne-Guillemin, *Ormazd et Ahriman*. It seems, however, that
   Duchesne-Guillemin later changed his position; see his view in *The
   Western Response to Zoroaster*.
5 Gershevitch, *The Avestan Hymn to Mithra*, 8–22.
6 Kent, *Old Persian Grammar*, 132, DBIV lines 59–64; and 138, DNa lines
   1–8.
7 Kent, *Old Persian Grammar*, 151–2, XPh lines 13–56. For the Akkadian
   version of this text, see Pritchard, ed., *Ancient Near Eastern Texts
   Relating to the Old Testament*, 316.
8 Kent, *Old Persian Grammar*, 154, A2Sa lines 1–5; and 155, A2Hc lines 1–3.
9 Ibid., 132, DBIV lines 59–64.
10 Stronach, *Iran* (1963), 1, 29–41; (1965), 3: 24; Ghirshman, *L'Iran*, 160.
11 Schmidt, *Persepolis*, 2: 55.
12 Stronach, *Iran* (1965), 3: 24.
13 Some scholars (like Herzfeld and Parrot) maintain that the building
   served as a tomb; others (like Erdmann and Ghirshman) maintain

that the building was used as a fire-temple. Stronach, *Iran* III (1965): 14–17, disagrees with both views and suggests that the building was probably the sanctuary that Gaumata destroyed and Darius restored.

14 Stronach, *Iran* (1965), 3: 120, DBI lines 61–6.

15 Schmidt, *Persepolis* 2.

16 Schmidt, *Persepolis* (1953), 2: 117.

17 According to Strabo, *Geography*, XI.515, these nomads were the Parni, kinsmen of the Scythians who lived to the north of the Black Sea.

18 The Roman historian Trogus Pompeius (ca. CE 10) described Arshak as "a man of uncertain origin but undisputed bravery," quoted in Watson, *Justin, Cornelius Nepos, and Eutropius*, 275.

19 For a list of the names of the Arsacid kings see: Debevoise, *A Political History of Parthia*, 270; Parker and Dubberstein, *Babylonian Chronology 626 BC – AD 45*, 22.

20 Schoff, *Parthian Stations by Isidore of Charax*, no. 11, 9; no. 6, 7. The ruins of this temple of Anahita are believed to have been discovered at Kangavar, some distance from Ecbatana (modern Hamadan); see Pope, *A Survey of Persian Art from Prehistoric Times to the Present*, 1: 413.

21 See for instance Tacitus, *The Annals and the Histories*, 12.13; Dio Cassius, *Roman History*, 63.5.

22 So believed by Olmstead, "Intertestamental Studies," 253 n. 40; Debevoise, *A Political History of Parthia*, 27.

23 No collected work on the Armenian sources is available. The article of M.H. Ananikian, "Armenia (Zoroastrian)," 794–802, is still valuable but should be used with caution.

24 Agathangelos, *History*, 58–61, 106, 590–3, 623. Cf. rejection of Ahura Mazda in Moses of Khorene (Chorene), *History and Geography of Armenia*, i.31. The fatherhood of Ahura Mazda is not altogether foreign to the Avesta; see for instance Yasna 14.4, 34.10; Yasht 17.16.

25 Agathangelos, *History*, 590, 612; Moses of Khorene, *History and Geography of Armenia*, ii.77; cf. Bundahishn 17.5–6.

26 According to the calendar of pre-Christian Armenia, Navasard was celebrated in August by gathering, distributing, and eating the new autumn fruits.

27 For Iranian, including Zoroastrian, festivals celebrated in the Parthian period, see Boyce, "Iranian Festivals," 792–815.

28 For the problem of sources regarding Sasan and Papak, the immediate predecessors of Ardashir, see Frye's article , "The Political History of Iran Under The Sasanians," 116–18.

29 Wikander, *Feuerpriester in Kleinasien und Iran*, rejects the tradition which makes Ardashir founder of Mazdayasnian orthodoxy; on the other hand, Zaehner, *The Dawn and Twilight of Zoroastrianism*, contends that the Sasanid kings were forced to impose Mazdayasnian orthodoxy in response to the rising dogmatism of Christianity and Manichaeism.

When and by whom Mazdayasnianism became the state religion
are still unresolved matters.

30 Kartir's inscriptions are carved in royal fashion on the rock-face of
Naqsh-i-Rustam, on the smooth stone walls of the Ka'ba-yi-
Zardusht in Naqsh-i-Rustam, another at Naqsh-i-Rajab, and the longest
on a mountainside at Sar-Mashdad (south of Kazerum, close to
modern Pars). For a transliteration and translation of this inscription
see Gignoux, "L'Inscription de Kartir à Sar Mashad," 387–418.

31 On the biography of Mani, see: Klima, *Manis Zeit und Leben*; Ort, *Mani:
A Religio-Historical Description of His Personality*; Flügel, *Mani seine
Lehre und seine Schiften*.

32 On Manichaeism, see Widengren, *Mani and Manichaeism*; Asmussen,
"Manichaeism," 580–610; Widengren, "Manichaeism and Its Iranian
Background," 965–90; Puech, *Le Manichéisme: son fondateur, sa doctrine*;
Burkitt, *The Religion of the Manichees*.

33 The religion of Mani spread beyond the borders of Persia. On the spread
of Manichaeism to China, see: Maenchen-Helfen, "Manichaeans in
Siberia," 311–26; Bisson, "Some Chinese Records of Manichaeism in
China," 415–28. On the spread of Manichaeism in the
Mediterranean world and Europe, see Brown, "The Diffusion of
Manichaeism in the Roman Empire," 92–103; Runciman, *The
Medieval Manichee*; Russell, *Dissent and Reform in the Early Middle Ages*;
Lieu, *Manichaeism in the Later Roman Empire and Medieval China*.

34 See Braun, *Ausgewählte Akten Persischer Martyrer mit eint Anhang*, I.30,
67.

35 Hoffman, *Auszuge aus Syrischen Akten*, 39.

36 Ibid., 34–8.

37 Ibid., 42.

38 See, for instance, the writings (in Armenian) of Yeghisheh, Moses of
Khorene, and Faustus.

39 Nigosian, "Zoroastrianism in Fifth-century Armenia," 425–34; J.R.
Russell, *Zoroastrianism in Armenia*.

40 There are twenty-eight different editions of Yeghisheh's work in classical
Armenian. The *Antzevatziatz* edition is considered to be one of the
most authentic. Here, I have used Yeghisheh, *Yeghisheh, vasn Vardanants'
ew Hayots' Paterazmin*. For an English translation, see Thompson,
ed., *History of Vardan and the Armenian War*.

41 Yeghisheh, 18.

42 Ibid., 36–8.

43 Ibid., 34–6.

44 For a detailed analysis on Mazdak and the Mazdakites, consult the following: Yarshater, "Mazdakaism," 991–1024; H. Gaube, "Mazdak:
Historical Reality or Invention?" 111–22; Klima, *Beiträge zur Geschichte*

des Mazdakismus; Klima, *Mazdak: Geschichte einer sozialen Bewegung im sassanidischen Persien;* Altheim, "Mazdak and Porphyrios," 1–20; N.V. Pigulevskaia, *Goroda Irana,* French trans. *Les villes de l'État iranien aux époques parthe et sassanide,* 195–230; Molé, "Le problème des sectes Zoroastriennes dans les livres phelevis," 1–28; T. Nöldeke, "Orientalischer Socialismus," 284–91.

45 Frye, *The Heritage of Persia,* 250.

46 Colpe, "Development of Religious Thought," 863.

47 Ghirshman, *L'Iran,* 302.

48 Nöldeke, *Geschichte der Perser und Araber zur Zeit der Sasaniden,* 268.

49 For an account of Zoroastrian life in modern Sharifabad, Iran, see Boyce, *A Persian Stronghold of Zoroastrianism.* For a description of Zoroastrians in Yazd, Iran, see Jackson, *Persia Past and Present;* Browne, *A Year Amongst the Persians.* For problems of coexistence during the early Islamic period, see Choksy, "Zoroastrians in Muslim Iran," 17–30.

50 Bailey, *Zoroastrian Problems in the Ninth-Century Books.*

51 Firdausi, *Shah-nama of Firdausi.*

52 For a survey of European travellers to India (and Persia), see Menant, *Les Parsis, histoire des communautés zoroastriennes de l'Inde;* Kulke, *The Parsees in India,* 29–30.

53 Anklesaria, *The Pahlavi Rivayat of Aturfarnbag and Farnbag-Sros,* and Dhabhar, *The Persian Rivayats of Hormazyar Framarz and Others;* Hodivala, *Studies in Parsi History,* 276–349; Paymaster, *Early History of the Parsees in India,* 66–84.

54 Bahman Ibn Kai-Kubad, "Kisse Sanjan," 91–122; Hodivala, *Studies in Parsi History,* 92–117; M.S. Irani, *The Story of Sanjan.*

55 Bulsara, *Highlights of Parsi History,* 21.

56 For a brief discussion on these disputed issues, see: Kulke, *The Parsees in India,* 26–8; Nariman, "Was It Religious Persecution Which Compelled the Parsis to Migrate from Persia to India?" 277; Westergaard, *Zendavesta,* 1: 22.

57 For a bibliography on the Parsees, see Kulke, *The Parsees: A Bibliography on an Indian Minority;* Hinnells, "The Parsis: a bibliographical survey," 100–49.

58 Whitehurst, "The Zoroastrian Response to Westernization," 224–36; Axelrod, "Myth and Identity in the Indian Zoroastrian Community," 150–65; Hinnells, "Parsi and the British," 1–92; Pangborn, *Zoroastrianism: A Beleaguered Faith.*

CHAPTER THREE

1 The name Avesta has presently replaced the earlier erroneous designation of Zend-Avesta (*zend* or *zand* meaning "translation, commen-

tary" – an inversion of the proper order of the words) in order to prevent the propagation of error.

2 For more information see Geiger, ed., *Grundriss der Iranischen Philologie*, 2: 1–129; Tavadia, *Die mittelpersische Sprache und Literatur der Zarathustrier*; Gershevitch, "Old Iranian Literature," 1–30; Boyce, "Middle Persian Literature," 31–66.

3 Haug, *Essays on the Sacred Language*, 146, is considered to be the first individual to make this linguistic observation and to consider the Gathas as the only authentic utterances of Zoroaster.

4 Selections of Yasna 1, 2, 65, 71 are from Darmesteter and Mills, *The Zend-Avesta*, vol. 31, 195–206, 316–17, 327–8. Selections of Yasna 31, 43 are from Insler, *The Gathas of Zarathustra*, 37, 39, 61, 65.

5 Selections of Visparad 5, 15, 23 are from Darmesteter and Mills, *The Zend-Avesta*, 31: 344–5, 357, 363–4.

6 E. Benveniste, "Que signifie Videvdat?" 37–42.

7 Boyce, "Parthian Writings and Literature," 1159.

8 Selections of Videvdat III, V, VII, VIII, XVI, are from Darmesteter and Mills, *The Zend-Avesta*, 4: 26, 31, 57–8, 91–2, 185.

9 Selections of Gah I, V, Afringan Gahambar are from Darmesteter and Mills, *The Zend-Avesta*, 31: 379, 387, 372.

10 Selections of Yasht 1, 5, 10, 17 are from Malandra, *An Introduction to Ancient Iranian Religion*.

11 On literature written in Pahlavi, see Boyce, "Middle Persian Literature," 31–66; de Menasce, "Zoroastrian Pahlavi Writings", 1166–95; Gignoux, "Middle Persian Inscriptions," 1205–15.

12 de Menasce, "Zoroastrian Pahlavi Writings," 1169.

13 Choksy, "An Annotated Index of the Greater or Iranian Bundahisn (TD$_2$)," 203–42.

14 Selections of Bundahishn 1, 14 are from Anklesaria, *Zand-Akâsîh*, 2, 100.

15 Selections of Shayest ne-Shayest 2, 4, 6, 8, 10, 12 are from West, *Pahlavi Texts*, 5: 248, 261, 262, 265, 285, 288, 293, 300, 322, 395.

16 Selections of Shkand Gumanig Wizar 10, 11, 13, 15, 16 are from West, *Pahlavi Texts*, 24: 168–70, 173, 208–9, 216–17, 229–34, 243, 246.

17 Selections of Denkard 6 are from Shaked, *The Wisdom of the Sasanian Sages (Denkard VI)*, 55, 65, 85, 133, 135, 169, 177, 185, 199.

CHAPTER FOUR

1 On the concept of *menog* and *getig*, see Shaked, "The Notions of *mênôg* and *gêtig* in the Pahlavi Texts," 59–107.

2 On Vohu Manah's role, see the arguments put forward by Windführ, "Vohu Mana: A Key to the Zoroastrian World-Formula," 269–310.

3 On the role of Ahriman, see Shaked, "Some Notes on Ahreman, The Evil Spirit, and His Creation," 277–334.

4 The question of the origin of Ahura Mazda and Ahriman was raised and an answer found in Zurvan; see next section in the text.

5 For instance, see the work of Zaehner, *Zurvan: A Zoroastrian Dilemma*.

6 Yeghisheh, *Yeghisheh, vasn Vardanants' ew Hayots' Paterazmin*, 34–8.

7 The Zoroastrian moral triad of purity and impurity of thought, word, and deed has been immortalized in the prayer recited by every devout Armenian Christian each time she or he enters the church: "O Jesus, Wisdom of the Father! Grant me wisdom, that I may always think, speak, and do that which is good in Thy sight. Save me from evil thoughts, words, and deeds ..."

8 Almost every feature of this picture may be paralleled in Christianity and Islam; see Matt. 24:3–31; Rev. 20:12–21:5; Qur'an 69.14–35.

9 The scholarly discussions on the influence of Zoroastrianism on Judaism, Christianity, and Islam are extensive. See for instance: Neusner, *Judaism, Christianity, and Zoroastrianism in Talmudic Babylonia*; Barr, "The Question of Religious Influence," 201–35; Shaked, "Iranian Influence on Judaism," 308–25; Hinnells, "Zoroastrian Influence on the Judaeo-Christian Tradition," 1–23; Hinnells, "Zoroastrian Saviour Imagery and Its Influence on the New Testament," 161–85; Winston, "The Iranian Component in the Bible, Apocrypha and Qumran," 183–216; Smith, "II Isaiah and the Persians," 415–21; Carter, *Zoroastrianism and Judaism*.

10 For a general treatment of the problems, see Duchesne-Guillemin, *The Western Response to Zoroaster*, and *La Religion de l'Iran Ancien*; E. Yarshater, "Introduction," lxv-lxxv.

11 Those who maintain Zoroastrian influence are: Shaked, "Iranian Influence on Judaism," 308–25; Hinnells, "Zoroastrian Influence," 1–23; Carter, *Zoroastrianism and Judaism*; Boyce, *Zoroastrians: Their Religious Beliefs and Practices*.

12 Those who reject Zoroastrian influence are: Barr, "The Question of Religious Influence," 201–35; Hanson, *The Dawn of Apocalyptic*; Jones, "The Manual of Discipline (1QS), Persian Religion, and the Old Testament."

13 Shaked, "Iranian Influnce on Judaism," 324.

CHAPTER FIVE

1 Translation by Choksy, *Purity and Pollution in Zoroastrianism*, 139.

2 *The Order of Baptism According to the Rite of the Armenian Apostolic Orthodox Church*, (Anon. New York: Armenian Prelacy, 1976), 15–19.

3 Ibid.
4 Ibid.
5 Translation by Choksy, *Purity and Pollution in Zoroastrianism*, 139.
6 Ibid., 139, 143. For other renderings, see: Boyce (1984), Hinnells (1981), and Malandra (1983).
7 The most recent study is that of Choksy, *Purity and Pollution in Zoroastrianism*. Consult the works of Mary Boyce for valuable studies on the subject. For a detailed scholarly description, see Modi, *The Religious Ceremonies and Customs of the Parsees*.
8 Boyce, *A Persian Stronghold of Zoroastrianism*, 112.
9 Choksy, *Purity and Pollution in Zoroastrianism*, 42.
10 Boyce, *A Persian Stronghold of Zoroastrianism*, 137–8.
11 For an interpretation of the Yasna, see Darrow, "Keeping the Waters Dry," 417–42; Windführ, "The Word in Zoroastrianism," 133–78.
12 Kotwal and Boyd, "The Zoroastrian *Paragnā* Ritual," 18–52.
13 On the fire cult, see Boyce, "On the Sacred Fires of Zoroastrianism," 52–68; Boyce, "On the Zoroastrian Temple Cult of Fire," 454–65; Kotwal, "Some Observations on the History of the Parsi *Dar-i Mihr*," 664–9.
14 The sanctity and veneration of fire is depicted on the reverse coins of the Sasanids, which bore the image of a fire-altar and flames, often tended by two priests. Examples of these coins are reproduced in Göbl, *Sasanian Numismatics*.
15 Among other literature, see Whitehurst, "The Zoroastrian Response to Westernization," 224–36; Axelrod, "Myth and Identity in the Indian Zoroastrian Community," 150–65; Kulke, *The Parsees in India*; Hinnells, "Parsi and the British," 1–92; Pangborn, *Zoroastrianism: A Beleaguered Faith*; du Breuil, *Le zoroastrisme*; Homji, *Zoroastrianism*.
16 Gould, "Parsis and Urban Demography," 345–52; Chandra, "Some Aspects of Parsi Demography," 47–89; Desai, *A Community at the Crossroad*; Gustafson, "A Demographic Dilemma," 115–27.
17 From a Pahlavi treatise entitled "Selected Counsels of the Ancient Sages," in Zaehner, *The Teachings of the Magi*.
18 From Shkand Gumanig Wizar 10.43–60 in Zaehner, *The Teachings of the Magi*, 52.

Bibliography

Spelling variations often occur in the transcriptions of titles of Zoroastrian texts.

Standard editions and translations of the Avesta and other Zoroastrian documents can be found under the following entries:

For Avesta, see:
  Barr, Darmesteter, Darmesteter and Mills, Geldner, Schlerath, Westergaard, Wolff.
For Gathas, see:
  Bartholomae, Bode, Chatterjee, Duchesne-Guillemin, Humbach, Insler, Lentz, Lommel, Markwart, Monna, Smith.
For Yashts and fragments of Avesta, see:
  Geldner, Gershevitch, Hertel, Lommel, Malandra, Narten, Wang, Wikander.
For other Zoroastrian documents, see:
  Anklesaria, Asa and Haug and West, Boyce, Chacha, de Menasce, Dhabhar, Dresden, Gignoux, Humbach, Jamasp, Jamasp-Asana, Kotwal, Madan, Modi, Molé, Shaked, Tavadia, Unvala, West.

Agathangelos. *History*. Venice: St. Lazar Edition, Venice 1892.
al-Baladhuri. *Ansab al-ashraf*. Edited and translated by M. Hamidullah. Vol. 1. Cairo: Dar al-Ma'arif 1959.
al-Biruni. *The Chronology of Ancient Nations*. Edited and translated by C.E. Sachau. London: William H. Allen 1879; reprint Hijra International 1983.
al-Bukhari. *Kitab al-jami' as-sahih*. 4 vols. Edited and translated by M.L. Krehl and T.W. Juynboll. Leiden: E.J. Brill 1862–1908.
Altheim, Franz. "Mazdak and Porphyrios." *History of Religions* (1963) 3: 1–20.

Ammianus Marcellinus. *History*. 12 vols. Edited and translated by John C. Rolfe. Loeb Classical Library. London: William Heineman 1950–52.

Ananikian, M.H. "Armenia (Zoroastrian)." In *Encyclopaedia of Religion and Ethics*, Edited by J. Hastings, 1: 794–802. Edinburgh: University of Edinburgh 1924.

Anklesaria, Behramgore T. *Pahlavi Vendidad*. Bombay: K.R. Cama Oriental Institute 1949.

– *Zand Akâsîh, Iranian or Greater Bundahisn*. Bombay: Rahnumae Mazdasna Sabha 1956.

– *Zand-i Vohuman Yasn and Two Pahlavi Fragments*. Bombay: K.L. Bargava 1957.

– *Rivayat-i Hemit-i Asavahistan, I*. Bombay: K.R. Cama Oriental Institute 1962.

– *Vichitakiha-i Zatsparam, I*. Bombay: Panchayet 1964.

– *The Pahlavi Rivayat of Aturfarnbag and Farnbag-Sros, 2v. I*. Bombay: M.F. Cama Athornan Institute 1969.

Anklesaria, Tahmuras D. *The Datistan-i-Dinik*. Bombay: Fort Printing Press 1899.

– *The Bundahishn*. Bombay: British India Press 1908.

– *Madigan-i-Hazar Dadistan, II*. Bombay: Fort Printing Press 1913.

Anonymous. *The Order of Baptism According to the Rite of the Armenian Apostolic Orthodox Church*. New York: Armenian Prelacy 1976.

Asa, Hoshang J., Martin Haug, and E.W. West. *Arda Viraf Namag*. Amsterdam: Oriental Press 1971; (orig. London 1872).

Asmussen, Jes Peter. "Manichaeism." *Historia Religionum*, edited by C.J. Bleeker and Geo Widengren, 1: 580–610. Leiden: E.J. Brill 1969.

at-Tibrizi. *Mishkat al-Masabih*. 4 vols. Edited and translated by J. Robson. Lahore: M. Ashraf 1963–65.

Axelrod, Paul. "Myth and Identity in the Indian Zoroastrian Community." *Journal of Mithraic Studies* 3/1–2 (1980): 150–65.

Bahman Ibn Kai-Kubad. "Kisse Sanjan, or The Story of Sanjan." In *The Story of Sanjan; or The Supposed History of the Parsi Migration to India from Khorasan. A Critical Study*, edited and translated by Mehrban Sohrab Irani, 91–122. Poona: M.S. Irani 1943.

Bailey, Harold W. *Zoroastrian Problems in the Ninth-Century Books*. Oxford: Oxford University Press 1943; reprint 1971.

Barbier de Meynard, C. *Dictionnaire géographique, historique et littéraire de la Perse et des contrées adjacentes extrait du Mo'djem el Bouldan de Yagout, et complété à l'aide de documents arabes et persans pour la plupart inédits*. Paris: Imprimerie Impériale 1861.

Barr, James. "The Question of Religious Influence: The Case of Zoroastrianism, Judaism, and Christianity." *Journal of the American Academy of Religion* 53/2 (1985): 201–35.

Barr, Kaj. *Avesta oversat og forklaret*. Copenhagen: F.S. Mule 1954.

Bartholomae, Christian. *Die Gatha's des Awesta*. Strassburg: K.J. Trubner 1905.

– *Zarathustra's Leben und Lehre*. Heidelberg: C. Winter 1924.

Belenitsky, A. *The Ancient Civilization of Central Asia*. London: Barrie and Rockliff, The Cresset Press 1969.

Benveniste, Émile. *The Persian Religion According to the Chief Greek Texts*. Paris: P. Geuthner 1929.

– *Les Mages dans l'ancien Iran*. Paris: G.P. Maisonneuve 1938.

– "Que signifie Videvdat?" In *W.B. Henning Memorial Volume*, edited by Mary Boyce and Ilya Gershevitch. 37–42. London: Lund Humphries 1970.

Beskow, Per. "The Routes of Early Mithraism." In *Études Mithraiques*, 7–18. Acta Iranica 17. Leiden: E.J. Brill 1978.

Bianchi, Umberto. *Il dualismo religioso; saggio, storico et etnologico*. Rome: L'Erma di Bretschneider 1958.

Bisson, T.A. "Some Chinese Records of Manichaeism in China." *The Chinese Recorder* 60 (1929): 415–28.

Bode, Framroze A. *Man, Soul and Immortality in Zoroastrianism*. Bombay: Mehta Education Trust 1960.

Bode, Framroze A. and Piloo Nanavutty. *The Songs of Zarathushtra, The Gathas*. Ethical and Religious Classics of East and West. London: G. Allen [and] Unwin 1952.

Bosch-Gimpera, P. "The Migration Route of the Indo-Aryans." *Journal of Indo-European Studies* 1 (1973): 513–17.

Boyce, Mary. "*Atas-zohr* and *Ab-zohr*." *Journal of the Royal Asiatique Society* (1966): 100–18.

– *The Letter of Tansar (Tansar Name)*. Rome Oriental Series 38. Rome: Istituto Italiano per il Medio ed Estremo Oriente 1968.

– "Middle Persian Literature." *Iranistik* Lfg. 1 (1968): 31–66.

– "On the Sacred Fires of the Zoroastrians." *Bulletin of the School of Oriental and African Studies* 31/1 (1968): 52–68.

– "The Pious Foundations of the Zoroastrians." *Bulletin of the School of Oriental and African Studies* 31/2 (1968): 270–89.

– "Haoma Priest of the Sacrifice." In *W.B. Henning Memorial Volume*, edited by Mary Boyce and Ilya Gershevitch, 62–80. London: Lund Humphries 1970.

– "On the Calendar of Zoroastrian Feasts." *Bulletin of the School of Oriental and African Studies* 33/3 (1970): 513–39.

– "Zoroaster the Priest." *Bulletin of the School of Oriental and African Studies* 33/1 (1970): 22–38.

– "Zoroastrian *Baj* and *Dron*-II." *Bulletin of the School of Oriental and African Studies* 34/2 (1971): 298–313.

– *A History of Zoroastrianism.* 2 vols. Leiden: E.J. Brill. Vol. 1 1975; reprint 1989; Vol. 2 1982.
– "On the Zoroastrian Temple-cult of Fire." *Journal of the American Oriental Society* 90/3 (1975): 454–65.
– *A Persian Stronghold of Zoroastrianism.* Oxford: Oxford University Press 1977.
– *Zoroastrians: Their Religious Beliefs and Practices.* London: Routledge and Kegan Paul 1979.
– "Iranian Festivals." In *The Cambridge History of Iran,* edited by Ehsan Yarshater, 3(2): 792–815. Cambridge: Cambridge University Press 1983.
– "Parthian Writings and Literature." In *The Cambridge History of Iran,* edited by Ehsan Yarshater, 3(2): 1151–65. Cambridge: Cambridge University Press 1983.
– *Textual Sources for the Study of Zoroastrianism.* Manchester: Manchester University Press 1984.
Boyce, Mary and Firoze M. Kotwal. "Zoroastrian *Baj* and *Dron*-I." *Bulletin of the School of Oriental and African Studies* 34/1 (1971): 56–73.
Boyd, James W. and Donald A. Crosby. "Is Zoroastrianism Dualistic or Monotheistic?" *Journal of the American Academy of Religion* 47/4 (1979): 557–88.
Braun, O. *Ausgewählte Akten Persischer Martyrer mit einem Anhang.* Bibliothek der Kirchenväter 22. Kempten/Munichen: J. Kosel 1915.
Brough, John. "Soma and Amanita Muscaria." *Bulletin of the School of Oriental and African Studies* 34 (1971): 331–62.
Brown, P. "The Diffusion of Manichaeism in the Roman Empire." *Journal of Roman Studies* 59 (1969): 92–103.
Browne, Edward G. *A Year Amongst the Persians.* London: A. & C. Black 1893; reprint 1959.
Bulsara, Jal Feerose. *Highlights of Parsi History.* Bombay: P.P. Bulsara 1963.
Burkitt, Francis C. *The Religion of the Manichees.* Cambridge: Cambridge University Press 1925.
Burnouf, Eugène. *Commentaire sur le Yaçna.* Paris: Imprimerie Royale 1933.
Burrow, Thomas. "The Proto-Indoaryans." *Journal of the Royal Asiatic Society* (1973): 123–40.
Carrière, Auguste. *Nouvelles sources de Moïse de Khoren: études critiques supplément.* Vienne: Imprimerie des Mechitaristes 1894.
Carter, George W. *Zoroastrianism and Judaism.* Boston: R.C. Badger 1918; reprint AMS Press 1970.
Chacha, H.F. *Gajastak Abalis.* Bombay: Parsi Panchayet 1936.
Chandra C.S. "Some Aspects of Parsi Demography." *Human Biology* 20 (1948): 47–89.
Chatterjee, J.M. *The Hymns of Atharvan Zarathushtra.* Calcutta: Parsi Zoroastrian Association 1967.

Choksy, Jamsheed K. "An Annotated Index of the Greater or Iranian Bundahišn (TD₂)." *Studia Iranica* 15/2 (1986): 203–42.

- "Purity and Pollution in Zoroastrianism." *Mankind Quarterly* 27/2 (1986): 167–91.

- "The Zoroastrian Nahn Purification Rituals." *Journal of Ritual Studies* 1/2 (1987): 59–74.

- "Zoroastrians in Muslim Iran: Selected Problems of Coexistence and Interaction during the Early Medieval Period." *Iranian Studies* 20/1 (1987): 17–30.

- *Purity and Pollution in Zoroastrianism: Triumph over Evil*. Austin, Texas: University of Texas Press 1989.

Christensen, Arthur E. *Les Kayanides*. Copenhagen: Andr. Fred. Host 1931.

- *Die Iranier*. Handbuch der Altertumswissenschaft. Abt. 3 Tl.l. Bd.3. Munich: Kulturgeschichte des alten Orients 1933.

- *L'Iran sous les Sassanides*. 2nd ed. Copenhagen: E. Munksgaard 1944.

Clemen, Carl. *Die griechischen und lateinischen Nachrichten über die persische Religion*. Giessen: A. Töpelmann 1920.

- *Fontes historiae religionis Persicae*. Bonn: A. Marci et E. Weberi 1920.

Colpe, Carsten. "Development of Religious Thought." In *The Cambridge History of Iran*, edited by Ehsan Yarshater, 3(2): 819–65. Cambridge: Cambridge University Press 1983.

Dandamaev, Mukhammed A. *A Political History of the Achaemenid Empire*. Leiden: E.J. Brill 1989.

Darmesteter, James. *Le Zend-Avesta: traduction nouvelle avec commentaire historique et philologique*. 3 vols. Annales du Musée Guimet. Paris: Ernest Leroux 1892–3. Reprint, Delhi: Motilal Banarsidass, 1960.

Darmesteter, James and L.H. Mills. *The Zend Avesta*. Sacred Books of the East Series. Edited by Max Müller. Oxford: Oxford University Press vol. 4 1880, vol. 23 1883, vol. 31 1887; reprint Motilal Banarsidas 1965, 1969; Greenwood 1972.

Darrow, William R. "Keeping the Waters Dry. The Semiotics of Fire and Water in Zoroastrian *Yasna*." *Journal of the American Academy of Religion* 56/3 (1988): 417–42.

de Menasce, Pierre J. *Skand-Gumānīk Vičār: La Solution Décisive des Doutes*. Fribourg en Suisse: Libraire de l'Université 1945.

- *Dinkard* (Book III). Paris: C. Klincksieck 1973.

- "Zoroastrian Pahlavi Writings." *The Cambridge History of Iran*, edited by Ehsan Yarshater, 3(2): 1166–95. Cambridge: Cambridge University Press 1983.

Debevoise, Neilson C. *A Political History of Parthia*. Chicago: University of Chicago Press 1938.

Decret, Francois. *Mani et la tradition manichéenne*. Paris: Seuil 1974.

Desai, Sapur Faredun. *A Community at the Crossroad*. Bombay: New Book Co. 1948.

Dhabhar, Bamanji. N. *Saddar Nasr and Saddar Bundehesh: Persian Texts Relating to Zoroastrianism*. Bombay: Parsi Panchayet 1909.

– *The Epistles of Manushchihar*. Bombay: Fort Printing Press 1912.

– *Pahlavi Rivayats Accompanying the Dadistan-i Dinik*. Bombay: K.R. Cama Oriental Institute 1913.

– *Zand-i Khurtak Avistak*. Bombay: Parsi Panchayet 1927.

– *The Persian Rivayats of Hormazyar Framarz and Others*. Bombay: K.R. Cama Oriental Institute 1932.

– *Pahlavi Yasna and Visperad*. Bombay: Shahnamah Press 1949.

Dhalla, Maneckji N. *Zoroastrian Civilization from the Earliest Times to the Downfall of the Last Zoroastrian Empire, 651 A.D*. New York: Oxford University Press 1922.

– *History of Zoroastrianism*. New York: Oxford University Press 1938; reprint K.R. Cama Oriental Institute 1963.

– *The Nyaishes or Zoroastrian Litanies; Avestan Text with the Pahlavi, Sanskrit, Persian and Gujarat*. New York: AMS Press 1965.

– *Zoroastrian Theology From the Earliest Times to the Present Day*. New York: np. 1914; reprint AMS Press 1972.

Diakonoff, I.M. "Media." In *The Cambridge History of Iran*, edited by Ilya Gershevitch, 2: 36–148. Cambridge: Cambridge University Press 1985.

Dio Cassius. *Roman History*. 9 vols. Loeb Classical Library no. 53, London: W. Heinemann, 1914–27.

Dresden, Mark J. *Denkart: A Pahlavi Text*. Wiesbaden: O. Harrassowitz 1966.

du Breuil, Paul. *Zarathoustra (Zoroastre) et la transfiguration du monde*. Paris:

Payot 1978.

– *Le zoroastrisme*. Paris: Presses Universitaires de France 1982.

– *Histoire de la religion et de la philosophie zoroastriennes*. Monaco: Édition de Rocher 1984.

Duchesne-Guillemin, Jacques. *Zoroastre*. Paris: G.P. Maisonneuve 1948.

– *Zoroastre, Étude critique avec une traduction commentée des Gatha*. Paris: G.P. Maisonneuve 1948.

– *The Hymns of Zarathustra*. Wisdom of the East Series. London: J. Murray, 1952. Reprint Westport, Connecticut: Hyperion Press 1979.

– *Ormazd et Ahriman. L'Aventure dualiste dans l'Antiquité*. Paris: Presses Universitaires de France 1953.

– *The Western Response to Zoroaster*. Oxford: Oxford University Press 1958; reprint Greenwood Press 1973.

– *Symbols and Values in Zoroastrianism*. New York: Harper & Row 1966; reprint 1970.

– *La Religion de l'Iran ancien*. Paris: Presses Universitaires de France 1962. English translation: *Religion of Ancient Iran*. Bombay: Tata Press 1973.

Dumézil, Georges. *Les dieux des indo-européens*. Paris: Presses Universitaires de France 1952.

Faustus. Lauer, Max. *Des Faustus von Byzanz Geschichte Armeniens, aus dem Armenischen übersetzt und mit einer Abhandlung über die Geographie Armeniens*. Köln: M. du Mont-Schauberg, 1879.

Firdausi. *Shah-nama of Firdausi*. 9 vols. Edited and translated by A.G. Warner and E. Warner. London: Trubner 1905–25.

Flügel, Gustav. *Mani seine Lehre und seine Schiften ein Beitrag zur Geschichte des Manichaismus, aus dem Fihrist des Abû'l faradsch Muhammad b. Ishak al Warrâk bekannt unter dem Namen Ibn Abî Ja'kûb an-Nadîm*. Leipzig: F.A. Brockhaus 1862.

Fox, Douglas "Darkness and Light: The Zoroastrian View." *Journal of the American Academy of Religion* 35 (1967): 129–37.

Fox, W.S. and R.E.K. Pemberton. *Passages in Greek and Latin Literature Relating to Zoroaster and Zoroastrianism, Translated into English*. Journal of the K.R. Cama Oriental Institute 14. Bombay: K.R. Cama Oriental Institute 1929.

Frumkin, Gregoire. *Archaeology in Soviet Central Asia*. Handbuch der Orientalistik VII.3.1. Leiden: E.J. Brill 1970.

Frye, Richard N. *The Heritage of Persia*. London: Weidenfeld and Nicholson 1963.

– "The Middle Persian Inscription of Kartir at Naqs-i Rajab." *Indo-Iranian Journal* 8 (1964): 211–25.

– "The Political History of Iran Under the Sasanians." *The Cambridge History of Iran* edited by Ehsan Yarshater, 3(1): 116–80. Cambridge: Cambridge University Press 1983.

– *The History of Ancient Iran*. Munich: C.H. Beck 1984.

– "Religion in Fars under the Achaemenids." In *Orientalia J. Duchesne-Guillemin Emerito Oblata*, 171–78. Acta Iranica 23. Leiden: E.J. Brill 1984.

Gaube, H. "Mazdak: Historical Reality or Invention?" *Studia Iranica* 2 (1982): 111–22.

Geiger, Wilhelm. ed. *Grundriss der Iranischen Philologie*. 2 vols. Strassbourg: K.J. Trubner 1895–1904.

Geldner, Karl F. *Drei Yasht aus dem Zendavesta*. Stuttgart: W. Kohlhammer 1884.

– *Avesta: The Sacred Books of the Parsis*. 3 vols. Stuttgart: W. Kohlhammer 1886–1895.

– *Die zoroastrische Religion (das Avesta)*. Tubingen: J.C.B. Mohr 1926.

Gershevitch, Ilya. *The Avestan Hymn to Mithra*. Cambridge: Cambridge University Press 1959; reprint 1967.

– "Zoroaster's Own Contribution." *Journal of Near Eastern Studies* 23/1 (1964): 12–38.

– "Old Iranian Literature." *Iranistik* Lfg. 1 (1968): 1–30.

– "An Iranist's View of the Soma controversy." In *Memorial Jean de Menasce*, edited by P. Gignoux and A. Taffazzoli, 45–75. Louvain: Imprimerie Orientaliste 1974.

Gershevitch, Ilya and Mary Boyce. "Middle Persian Literature." *Iranistik* 2 (1968): 31–66.

Ghirshman, Roman. *L'Iran et la migration des Indo-aryens et des Iraniens.* Leiden: E.J. Brill 1977.

Gignoux, M.Philippe. "L'Inscription de Kartir a Sar Mashad." *Journal Asiatique* (1969): 387–418.

– "Middle Persian Inscriptions." *The Cambridge History of Iran,* edited by Ehsan Yarshater, 3(2): 1205–15. Cambridge: Cambridge University Press 1983.

– *Le Livre d'Arda Viraz.* Paris: Editions Recherche sur les Civilisations 1984.

Gnoli, Gherardo. *Zoroaster's Time and Homeland.* Seminario di Studi Asiatici, Series Minor, vol. 7. Naples: Istituto Universitario Orientale 1980.

Göbl, Robert. *Sasanian Numismatics.* Translated by P. Severin. Brunswick: Klinkhardt and Biermann 1971.

Godbey, Allen H. "Incense and Poison Ordeals in the Ancient Orient." *American Journal of Semitic Languages and Literatures* 46 (1930): 221.

Gottheil, Richard J.H. "References to Zoroaster in Syriac and Arabic Literature." In *Classical Studies in Honour of Henry Drisler,* 24–51. New York: Macmillan 1894.

Gould, K.H. "Parsis and Urban Demography: Some Research Possibilities." *Journal of Marriage and the Family,* 34 (1972): 345–52.

Gray, Louis H. *The Foundations of the Iranian Religions.* Bombay: K.R. Cama Oriental Institute 1929.

Gustafson, E.B. "A Demographic Dilemma: The Parsis of Karachi." *Social Biology* 16 (1969): 115–27.

Haarbrucker, Theodor. *Abu-'l-Fath' Muhammad asch-Schahrastani' Religionspartheien und Philosophen-Schulen zum ersten Male vollständig aus dem Arabischen übersetz und mit erklärenden Anmerkungen versehen.* 2 vols. Hildesheim: G. Olms 1969; (orig. Halle 1850–1851).

Halkin, A.H. *Moslem Schisms and Sects.* Pt 2. Tel Aviv: Palestine Publishing 1935.

Hanson, Paul D. *The Dawn of Apocalyptic.* Philadelphia: Fortress Press 1975.

Hartman, Sven S. *Gayomart: étude sur le syncrétisme dans l'ancien Iran.* Uppsala: Almquist & Wiksell 1953.

– *Parsism. The Religion of Zoroaster.* Iconography of Religions 14/4. Leiden: E.J. Brill 1980.

Haug, Martin. *Essays on the Sacred Language, Writings and Religion of the Parsis.* 4th ed. London: Kegan Paul, Trench, Trubner & Co. Ltd. 1907.

Henning, Walter B. *Zoroaster, Politician or Witch-Doctor?* Oxford: Oxford University Press 1951.

Herodotus. *The Histories.* 4 vols. Translated by A.D. Godley. Loeb Classical Library. London: William Heinemann 1920–1924.

Hertel, Johanes. *Die Zeit Zoroasters.* Indo-iranische Quellen und Forschungen, Heft 1. Leipzig: S. Hirzel 1924.

– *Die awestische Herrschaft und Siegesfeuer.* Leipzig: S. Hirzel 1931.
– *Die Sonne und Mithra im Awesta.* Leipzig: S. Hirzel 1931.
– *Yashts.* Leipzig: S. Hirzel 1931.
Herzfeld, Ernest. *Paikuli, Monument and Inscription of the Early History of the Sassanian Empire.* 2 vols. Berlin: D. Reimer 1924.
– "The Iranian Religion at the Time of Darius and Xerxes." *Religions* 15 (1936): 20–8.
– *Altpersische Inschriften.* Berlin: D. Reimer 1938.
– *Zoroaster and His World.* 2 vols. Princeton: Princeton University Press 1947; reprint Octagon Books 1974.
Hinnells, John R. "Zoroastrian Saviour Imagery and Its Influence on the New Testament." *NUMEN* 16 (1969): 161–85.
– "Zoroastrian Influence on the Judaeo-Christian Tradition." *Journal of the K.R. Cama Oriental Institute* 45 (1976): 1–23.
– "Parsi and the British." *Journal of the K.R. Cama Oriental Institute* 46 (1978): 1–92.
– "The Parsis: A Bibliographical Survey." *Journal of Mithraic Studies.* 3/1–2 (1980): 100–49.
– *Zoroastrianism and the Parsis.* London: Ward Lock Educational 1981.
Hinz, Walter. *Zarathusthtra.* Stuttgart: W. Köhlhammer 1961.
Hodivala, Shahpurshah H. *Studies in Parsi History.* Bombay: Bahauddin College 1920.
Hoffmann, G. *Auszuge aus Syrischen Akten Persischer Martyrer.* Leipzig: F.A. Brockhaus 1880; reprint 1966.
Homji, Homi B.M. *Zoroastrianism. Contemporary Perception of Ancient Wisdom.* Toronto: np. 1989.
Humbach, Helmut. *Die Gathas des Zarathustra,* 2 vols. Heidelberg: C. Winter 1959.
– *The Sassanian Inscriptions of Paikuli.* 2 vols. Wiesbaden: Reichert 1978–1983.
– "About Gopatsah, His Country, and the Khwarezmian Hypothesis." In *Papers in Honor of Professor Mary Boyce,* 327–34. Acta Iranica 24. Leiden: E.J. Brill 1985.
Humbach, Helmut and Kaikhusroo M. Jamaspasa. *Vaeda Nask: An Apocryphal Text on Zoroastrian Problems.* Wiesbaden: O. Harrassowitz 1969.
Insler, Stanley. *The Gathas of Zarathustra.* Acta Iranica 8. Leiden: E.J. Brill 1975.
Irani, Kaikhosrov D. "Reflections on the Zoroastrian Religion: The Philosophy of Belief and Practice." *Parsiana* 3/8 (1980): 13–23, 43–51.
Irani, Merwan Sorab. *The Story of Sanjan.* Poona: M.S. Irani 1943.
Jackson, A.V. Williams. *Zoroaster, The Prophet of Ancient Iran.* New York: Macmillan 1899; reprint AMS Press 1965.
– *Persia Past and Present, a Book of Travel and Research.* New York: Macmillan 1906.
– *Zoroastrian Studies.* New York: Columbia University Press 1928.

Jamasp, Hoshang. *Vendidad*. 2 vols. Bombay: Government Central Book Depot 1907.

Jamasp-Asana, Jamaspji M. *The Pahlavi Texts*. Bombay: Fort Printing Press 1913.

Jones, R.G. "The Manual of Discipline (1QS), Persian Religion, and the Old Testament." In *The Teacher's Yoke: Studies in Memory of Henry Trantham*, edited by E.J. Vardaman and J.L. Garrett. Waco, Texas: Baylor University Press 1964.

Karaka, Dosabhai F. *History of the Parsis: Including Their Manners, Customs, Religion, and Present Position*. 2 vols. London: Macmillan 1884.

Kent, Roland G. *Old Persian Grammar, Texts, Lexicon*, 2nd. ed. Newhaven: American Oriental Society 1953.

King, L.W., R.C. Thompson, and E.A. Budge. *The Sculptures and Inscription of Darius the Great on the Rock of Behistun in Persia*. London: Longmans 1907.

Kingsley, P. "The Greek Origin of the Sixth Century Dating of Zoroaster." *Bulletin of the School of Oriental and African Studies* 53 (1990): 245–65.

Klima, Otakar. *Mazdak: Geschichte einer sozialen Bewegung im sassanidischen Persien*. Prague: Nakladatelstvi, Československá akademie věd 1957.

– "The Date of Zoroaster." *Archiv Orientalní* 27 (1959): 556–64.

– *Manis Zeit und Leben*. Prague: Tschechoslowakische Akademie der Wissenschaften 1962.

– *Beiträge zur Geschichte des Mazdakismus*. Prague: Tschechoslowakische Akademie der Wissenschaften 1977.

Kotwal, Firoze M. *The Supplementary Texts to the Sayest ne-sayest*. Copenhagen: Munksgaard 1969.

– "Some Observations on the History of the Parsi Dar-i Mihr." *Bulletin of the School of Oriental and African Studies* 37 (1974): 664–9.

Kotwal, Firoze M. and James W. Boyd. "The Zoroastrian *Paragnā* Ritual." *Journal of Mithraic Studies* 2/1 (1977): 18–52.

Kotwal, Firoze M. and James W. Boyd. ed. *A Guide to the Zoroastrian. A Nineteenth Century Catechism with Modern Commentary*. Studies in World Religions 3. Chico, California: Scholars Press 1982.

Kreyenbroek, G. *Sraosa in the Zoroastrian Tradition*. Leiden: E.J. Brill 1985.

Kulke, Eckehard. *The Parsees: A Bibliography on an Indian Minority*. Freibourg: Arnold-Bargstraesser 1968.

– *The Parsees in India. A Minority as Agent of Social Change*. Delhi: Vikas Publishing House 1974.

Langlois, Victor. *Collection des historiens anciens et modernes de l'Arménie*. 2 vols. Paris: Imprimerie Nationale 1867–69.

Lentz, Wolfgang. *Yasna 28, Kommentierte Übersetzung und Kompositionsanalyse*. Wiesbaden: F. Steiner 1954.

Lieu, Samuel N.C. *Manichaeism in the Later Roman Empire and Medieval China: A Historical Survey*. Manchester: Manchester University Press 1985.

Lommel, Herman. *Die Yästs des Awesta*. Gottingen: Vandenhoeck & Ruprecht 1927.

– *Die Religion Zarathustras nach dem Awesta*. Tubingen: Mohr 1930.

– "Anahita-Sarasvati." In *Asiatica. Festschrift Friedrich Weller*, edited by J. Schubert and W. Schneider, 405–13. Leipzig: O. Harrassowitz 1954.

– *Zarathushtra's Priesterlohn*. Tubingen: Mohr 1955.

– *Zarathushtra und seine Lehre*. Tubingen: Mohr 1957.

– *Die Gathas des Zarathustra*. Basel: Schwabe 1971.

Madan, Dhanjishah M. *The Complete Text of the Pahlavi Dinkard*. 2 vols. Bombay: Society for the Promotion of Researches into the Zoroastrian Religion 1911.

Maenchen-Helfen, Otto J. "Manichaeans in Siberia." In *Semitic and Oriental Studies Presented to William Popper*, edited by W.J. Fischel. Berkley: University of California Press 1951.

Malandra, William W. *An Introduction to Ancient Iranian Religion: Readings from the Avesta and Achaemenid Inscriptions*. Minnesota Publications in the Humanities Series 2. Minneapolis, Minnesota: University of Minnesota Press 1983.

Markwart, J. and G. Messina. *Das erste Kapitel der Gatha Ustavati*. Rome: Pontificat Institutum Orientalium Studiorum 1930.

Masani, Rustom. *Zoroastrianism: The Religion of the Good Life*. New York: Macmillan 1938; reprint 1971.

Masson, Vadim M. and V.I. Sarianidi. *Central Asia, Turkmenia Before the Achaemenids*. London: Thames & Hudson 1972.

Maynard, C.B. and P. de Courteille. *Les prairies d'or*. 9 vols. Société asiatique, Collection d'ouvrages orientaux. Paris: Ch. Pellat 1962; (orig. 1861–77).

Mayrhofer, Manfred. *Die Indo-Arier im alten Vorderasien, mit einer analytischen Bibliographie*. Wiesbaden: O. Harrassowitz 1966.

Mehr, Farhang. *The Zoroastrian Tradition. An Introduction to the Ancient Wisdom of Zarathustra*. Rockport, Massachusetts: Element Inc. 1991.

Menant, D. *Les Parsis, histoire des communautés zoroastriennes de l'Inde*. Paris: E. Leroux 1898.

Mills, Lawrence H. *Zoroaster, Philo and Israel*. Leipzig: Brockhaus 1903.

– *Zarathustra, Philo, the Achaemenids and Israel*. Chicago: Open Court 1906.

Mistree, Khojeste P. *Zoroastrianism: An Ethnic Perspective*. Bombay: Zoroastrian Studies 1982.

Modi, Jivanji J. *Madigan-i-Hazar Dadistan*. Bombay: Parsi Panchayet 1901.

– *Jamaspi: Pahlavi, Pazend, and Persian Texts*. Bombay: Education Society 1903.

– *The Religious Ceremonies and Customs of the Parsees*. Bombay: British India Press 1922; reprint Garland 1980.

– *The Persian Farziat-Nameh and Kholaseh-i Din of Dastur Darab Pahlan*. Bombay: Fort Printing Press 1924.

Mohl, Julius. *Le Livre de Feridoun et de Minoutcher, roi de Perse*. Paris: L'édition d'art 1924.

Molé, Marijan. "Le problème des sectes zoroastriennes dans les livres pehlevis." *Oriens* 13–14 (1960–61): 1–28.

— *Culte, mythe et cosmologie dans l'Iran ancien*. Paris: Presses Universitaires de France 1963.

— *Le problème zoroastrien et la tradition mazdéenne*. Paris: Presses Universitaires de France 1963.

— *La légende Zoroastre selon les textes Pehlevis*. Paris: Librarie C. Klincksieck 1967.

Monna, Maria C. *The Gathas of Zarathustra: A Reconstruction of the Text*. Amsterdam: Rodopi 1978.

Moses of Khorene. *History and Geography of Armenia*. Venice: Edition Venice 1865.

Moulton, James Hope. *Early Zoroastrianism*. London: Williams and Norgate 1913; reprint Philo 1972.

— *The Teaching of Zarathushtra*. Bombay: Meherji B. Mithaiwala 1917.

— *The Treasure of the Magi. A Study of Modern Zoroastrianism*. London: H. Milford 1917; reprint AMS Press 1972.

Nanavutty, Piloo. *The Parsis*. New Delhi, India: National Book Trust 1977.

Nariman, Gushtaspshah K. "Was It Religious Persecution which Compelled the Parsis to Migrate from Persia to India?" *Islamic Culture* 7 (1933): 277.

Narten, Johanna. *Der Yasna Haptanhâiti*. Wiesbaden: Reichert 1986.

Neusner, Jacob. *Judaism, Christianity, and Zoroastrianism in Talmudic Babylonia*. Lanham, Maryland: University Press of America 1986.

Nigosian, Solomon A. "The Religions in Achaemenid Persia." *Studies in Religion* 4/4 (1974–75): 378–86.

— "Zoroastrianism in Fifth-century Armenia." *Studies in Religion* 7/4 (1978): 425–34.

Nöldeke, Theodor. *Geschichte der Perser und Araber zur Zeit der Sasaniden, aus der arabischen Chronik des Tabari übersetzt und mit ausführlichen Erlaüterungen und Ergänzungen versehn*. Leiden: E.J. Brill 1879.

— "Orientalischer Socialismus." *Deutsche Rundschau* 18 (1879): 284–91.

Nyberg, Henrik S. "Questions de cosmogonie et de cosmologie mazdéennes, II." *Journal Asiatique* 219 (1931): 1–134, 193–244.

— *Die Religionen des Alten Iran*. Leipzig: J.C. Hinrichs: 1938; reprint Zeller 1966.

Olmstead, Albert T. "Intertestamental Studies." *Journal of the American Oriental Society* 56, no. 2 (1936): 242–57.

— *History of the Persian Empire*. Chicago: University of Chicago Press 1948.

Oppert, Jules. *Les Inscriptions des Achéménides conçues dans l'idiome des anciens Perses*. Paris: Imprimerie Nationale 1851.

Ort, L.J.R. *Mani: A Religio-Historical Description of His Personality*. Leiden: E.J. Brill 1967.

Oxtoby, Willard G. "Interpretations of Iranian Dualism." In *Iranian Civilization and Culture: Essays in Honor of the 2500th Anniversary of the Persian Empire by Cyrus the Great*, edited by Charles J. Adams, 59–70. Montreal: McGill University, Institute of Islamic Studies 1972.

Pangborn, Cyrus R. *Zoroastrianism: A Beleaguered Faith*. New York: Advent Books 1983.

Parker, Richard A. and W.H. Dubberstein. *Babylonian Chronology 626 BC-AD 45*. Studies in Ancient Oriental Civilization 24. Chicago: University of Chicago Press 1942.

Pavry, J. Cursetji. *The Zoroastrian Doctrine of a Future Life: From Death to the Individual Judgment*. 2nd ed. New York: Columbia University Press 1926; reprint AMS Press 1965.

Paymaster, Rustom B. *Early History of the Parsees in India From Their Landing in Sanjan to 1700 A.D*. Bombay: Zarthoshti Dharam Sambandhi Kelavni Apnari ane Dnyan Felavnari Mandli 1954.

Pigulevskaia, Nina Victorovna. *Goroda Irana v rannem srednevekov'e*. Moscow-Leningrad, 1956. French translation, *Les villes de l'État iranien aux époques parthe et sassanide*. Paris: Mouton 1963.

Plato. *Alcibiades*. Translated by W.R.M. Lamb. Loeb Classical Library. London: William Heinemann 1927.

Pope, Arthur U, ed. *A Survey of Persian Art from Prehistoric Times to the Present*. 6 vols. London: Oxford University Press 1938–1939.

Pritchard, James B., ed. *Ancient Near Eastern Texts Relating to the Old Testament*. 3rd. ed. Princeton: Princeton University Press 1969.

Puech, Henri-Charles, *Le Manichéisme: son fondateur, sa doctrine*. Paris: Civilisation du Sud (S.A.E.P.) 1949.

Runciman, Steven. *The Medieval Manichee: A Study of the Christian Dualist Heresy*. Cambridge: Cambridge University Press 1947; reprint Viking Press 1961.

Russell, James R. *Zoroastrianism in Armenia*. Cambridge: Cambridge University Press 1987.

Russell, Jeffrey B. *Dissent and Reform in the Early Middle Ages*. Berkeley: University of California Press 1965.

Sanjana, P.B. and D.P. Sanjana, ed. and trans. *Dinkard*. 19 vols. Bombay: 1874–1928.

Schaeder, Hans Heinrich. "Zarathustras Botschaft von der rechten Ordnung." *Corona* 9 (1940): 575–602.

Scheftelowitz, Isidor. *Die altpersische Religion und das Judentum*. Giessen: Töpelmann 1920.

Schlerath, Bernfried. *Awesta-Wörterbuch Vorarbeiten II*. Wiesbaden: O. Harrassowitz 1968.

Schlerath, Bernfried, ed. *Zarathustra.* Wege der Forschung 169. Darmstadt: Wissenschaftliche Buchgesellschaft 1970.

Schmidt, Erich. F. *Persepolis, Structures, Reliefs, Inscriptions.* 2 vols. University of Chicago Oriental Institute Publications. Chicago: University of Chicago Press 1953–1970.

Schoff, Wilfred H. *Parthian Stations by Isidore of Charax. An Account of the Overland Trade Route Between the Levant and India in the First Century B.C. The Greek Text, with a Translation and Commentary.* np. 1914; reprint Ares 1989.

Schwartz, Martin. "The Old Eastern Iranian World View According to the Avesta." In *The Cambridge History of Iran,* edited by Ilya Gershevitch, 2: 640–63. Cambridge: Cambridge University Press 1985.

Seelye, Kate C. *Moslem Schisms and Sects.* Pt 1. New York: Columbia University Press 1920.

Shahbazi, A. Shapur. "The 'Traditional Date of Zoroaster' Explained." *Bulletin of the School of Oriental and African Studies* 40/1 (1977): 25–33.

Shaked, Shaul. "Some Notes on Ahreman, The Evil Spirit, and His Creation." In *Studies in Mysticism and Religion Presented to G.G. Sholem,* edited by C. Wirszubski, R.J.Z. Werblowsky, and E.E. Urbach. Jerusalem: Magnes Press, Hebrew University 1967.

– "The Notions of *mênôg* and *gêtig* in the Pahlavi Texts and Their Relation to Eschatology." *Acta Orientalia* 33 (1971): 59–107.

– "Qumran and Iran: Further Considerations." *Israel Oriental Studies* 2 (1972): 433–46.

– *The Wisdom of the Sasanian Sages (Denkard VI).* Persian Heritage Series 34. Boulder, Colorado: Westview Press 1979.

– *Irano-Judaica: Studies Relating to Jewish Contacts with Persian Culture.* Jerusalem: Ben-Zvi Institute for the Study of Jewish Communities in the East 1982.

– "Iranian Influence on Judaism: First Century B.C.E. to Second Century C.E." In *The Cambridge History of Judaism,* edited by W.D. Davies and L. Finkelstein, 1: 308–25. Cambridge: Cambridge University Press 1984.

Smith, Maria Wilkins. *Studies in the Syntax of the Gathas of Zarathushtra; together with Text, Translation and Notes.* Linguistic Society of America. Philadelphia: University of Pennsylvania 1929; reprint 1966.

Smith, Morton. "II Isaiah and the Persians." *Journal of the American Oriental Society* 83/4 (1963): 415–21.

Sprengling, Martin. *Third Century Iran, Sapor and Kartir.* Chicago: University of Chicago Press 1953.

Strabo. *The Geography of Strabo.* 8 vols. Translated by Horace L. Jones. Loeb Classical Library. London: William Heinemann 1917–32.

Stronach, David. *Iran.* 3 vols. Oxford: Oxford University Press 1963–1965.

– *Pasargadae.* Oxford: Clarendon Press 1978.

- "Notes on Religion in Iran in the Seventh and Sixth Centuries B.C.E." In *Orientalia J. Duchesne-Guillemin Emerito Oblata*, 479–90. Acta Iranica 23. Leiden: E.J. Brill 1984.

Tacitus. *The Annals and the Histories*. Translated by A.J. Church and W.J. Brodribb. New York: Twayne Publishers 1964.

Tardieu, Michel. *Le Manichéisme*. Paris: Presses Universitaires de France 1981.

Tavadia, Jehangir C. *Sayast-ne-sayast: A Pahlavi Text on Religious Customs*. Hamburg: Walter de Gruyter 1930.

- *Die mittelpersische Sprache und Literatur der Zarathustrier*. Leipzig: O. Harrassowitz 1956.

Thieme, Paul. "The Aryan gôds of the Mitani Treaties." *Journal of the American Oriental Society* 80/4 (1960): 301–17.

Thompson, Robert W., ed. and trans. *History of Vardan and the Armenian War*. Harvard Armenian Texts and Studies 5. Cambridge: Harvard University Press 1982.

Tiele, Cornelius P. *The Religion of the Iranian Peoples*. Bombay: British India Press 1912.

Tolman, Herbert C. *Ancient Persian Lexicon and Texts of the Achaemenidian Inscriptions*. The Vanderbilt Oriental Series 61. New York: American Book Co. 1908.

Unvala, Manockji. R. *Darab Hormazyar's Rivayats* 2 vols. Bombay: British India Press 1922.

Varenne, Jean. *Zoroastre*. Paris: Éditions Seghers 1975.

Vogelsang, W.J. *The Rise and Organisation of the Achaemenid Empire. The Eastern Iranian Tradition*. Leiden: E.J. Brill, 1992.

von Wesendonk, D.G. *Das Wesender Lehre Zarathushtra's*. Leipzig: O. Harrassowitz 1927.

- *Das Weltbild der Iranier*. München: E. Reinhart 1933.

Wang, Anatol. *Nirangistan, der Awestatraktat über die rituellen Vorschriften*. Iranische Forschungen, 2. Leipzig: J.C. Hinrichs 1941.

Wasson, R. Gordon. *Soma. Divine Mushroom of Immortality*. Ethnomycological Studies 1. New York: Harcourt Brace Jovanovich 1969.

- *Soma and the Fly-agaric: Mr Wasson's Rejoinder to Professor Brough*. Ethnomycological Studies 2. Cambridge, Massachusetts: Botanical Museum of Harvard University 1972.

Waterhouse, John W. *Zoroastrianism*. London: Epworth Press 1945.

Watson, John Selby, trans. *Justin, Cornelius Nepos, and Eutropius*. London: Bohn's Classical Library 1890.

West, Edward W. *The Book of the Mainyo-i-khard*. np. 1871; reprint APA-Oriental Press 1979.

- *Pahlavi Texts*. Sacred Books of the East Series, edited by Max Müller. Oxford: Oxford University Press, vol. 5 1880, vol. 24 1885; reprint Motilal Banarsidas 1965, 1970.

Westergaard, Niels L. *Zendavesta or The Religious Books of the Zoroastrians.* Copenhagen: F.S. Muhle 1852–54.

Whitehurst, J.E. "The Zoroastrian Response to Westernization: A Case Study of the Parsis of Bombay." *Journal of the American Academy of Religion* 37/3 (1969): 224–36.

Widengren, Geo. *Stand und Aufgaben der iranischen Religionsgeschichte.* Leiden: E.J. Brill 1955.

– *Mani and Manichaeism.* New York: Holt, Rinehart & Winston 1965.

– "Manichaeism and Its Iranian Background." In *The Cambridge History of Iran*, edited by Ehsan Yarshater, 3(2): 965–90. Cambridge: Cambridge University Press 1983.

Wikander, Oscar Stig. *Vayu; Texte und Untersuchungen zur indo-iranischen Religionsgeschichte.* Leipzig: O. Harrassowitz 1941.

– *Feuerpriester in Kleinasien und Iran.* Lund: C.W.K. Gleerup 1946.

Windführ, Gernot L. "Vohu Manah: A Key to the Zoroastrian World-Formula." In *Michigan Studies in Honor of George G. Cameron*, edited by L.L. Orlin, 269–310. Ann Arbor, Michigan: University of Michigan, Department of Near Eastern Studies 1976.

– "The Word in Zoroastrianism." *Journal of Indo-European Studies* 12/1–2 (1984): 133–78.

Winston, David. "The Iranian Component in the Bible, Apocrypha and Qumran: A Review of the Evidence." *History of Religion* 5/2 (1966): 183–216.

Wolff, Fritz. *Avesta, Die Heiligen Bücher der Parsen, übersetzt auf der Grundlage von Chr. Bartholomae's Altiranischen Wörterbuch.* Berlin: W. de Gruyter 1960; (orig. Strassburg 1910).

Xenophon. *Cyropaedia.* 2 vols. Translated by Walter Miller. Loeb Classical Library. London: William Heinemann 1914.

Yamauchi, Edwin M. *Persia and the Bible.* Grand Rapids: Baker Book House 1990.

Yarshater, Ehsan. "Introduction." In *The Cambridge History of Iran*, edited by Ehsan Yarshater, 3(1): lxv-lxxv. Cambridge: Cambridge University Press 1983.

– "Iranian Common Beliefs and World-View." In *The Cambridge History of Iran*, edited by Ehsan Yarshater, 3(1): 343–58. Cambridge: Cambridge University Press 1983.

– "Mazdakaism." In *The Cambridge History of Iran*, edited by Ehsan Yarshater, 3(2): 991–1024. Cambridge: Cambridge University Press 1983.

Yeghisheh. *Yeghisheh, vasn Vardanants ew Hayots Paterazmin.* Edited and translated by E. Ter-Minasean. Erevan, Armenia: University of Erevan 1989.

Young, T. Cuyler. "The Iranian Migration into the Zagros." *Iran* 5 (1967): 11–34.

Zaehner, Robert C. *Zurvan, A Zoroastrian Dilemma*. Oxford: Oxford University Press 1955; reprint Biblo and Tannen 1972.

– *The Teachings of the Magi: A Compendium of Zoroastrian Beliefs*. New York: Oxford University Press 1956; reprint 1976.

– *The Dawn and Twilight of Zoroastrianism*. New York: Putnam 1961.

– *Concordant Discord*. Oxford: Oxford University Press 1970.

Zotenberg, Hermann. *Chronique de Abou-Djafar-Mo'hammed-ben-Djari-ben Yezid Tabari: traduit sur la version persane d'Abou-'Ali Mohammed Bel'am*. 4 vols. Paris: G.P. Maisonneuve 1958; (orig. 1867–74).

Index